THE ELEGANT KNITTER

SIMPLE TECHNIQUES FOR
BEAUTIFUL RESULTS

THE ELEGANT KNITTER

SIMPLE TECHNIQUES FOR BEAUTIFUL RESULTS

HATS, SCARVES, GLOVES & MORE

GINA MACRIS

STERLING PUBLISHING CO., INC.
NEW YORK

Library of Congress Cataloging-in-Publication Data

Macris, Gina.
The elegant knitter : simple techniques for beautiful results; hats, scarves, gloves &
  more / Gina Macris.
p. cm.
ISBN-13: 978-1-4027-3992-7
ISBN-10: 1-4027-3992-3
1. Knitting—Patterns. I. Title.

TT825.M1548 2007
746.43'2041—dc22

2006052229

10 9 8 7 6 5 4 3 2 1

Published by Sterling Publishing Co., Inc.
387 Park Avenue South, New York, NY 10016

Created by Lynn Bryan, The BookMaker, London
Design by Carole Ash
Photography by Amanda Hancocks
US editor: Ellen Liberles
Pattern editor: Kate Buchanan

Distributed in Canada by Sterling Publishing
c/o Canadian Manda Group, 165 Dufferin Street,
Toronto, Ontario, Canada M6K 3H6

Distributed in the United Kingdom by GMC Distribution Services,
Castle Place, 166 High Street, Lewes, East Sussex, England BN7 1XU

Distributed in Australia by Capricorn Link (Australia) Pty. Ltd.
P.O. Box 704, Windsor, NSW 2756, Australia

Printed in China

Sterling ISBN-13: 978-1-4027-3992-7
          ISBN-10: 1-4027-3992-3

For information about custom editions, special sales, premium and
corporate purchases, please contact Sterling Special Sales Department at
800-805-5489 or specialsales@sterlingpub.com.

CONTENTS

Hats 41

A Chic Cloche 42

Scarves 55

A Child's Colorful
Cap 45

A Soft Baby Hat 48

Perfect Pom-Poms
51

A Dreamy Spiral
Scarf 56

Focus on Fringe 61

Big In Style 63

Beautiful Boucle 66

A Shibori Scarf 68

Medallion Motif for a Man's Scarf 72

A Creamy Cable Scarf 76

A Luscious Lacy Scarf 81

Modern Muffatees 86

Wow-Factor Dog Sweater 91

Glamorous Leg Warmers 96

A Fair Isle Dog Sweater 99

A Soft Band of Roses 102

Gloves 106

Accessorize with Color 105

Gorgeous Gloves 110

Kids' Stuff 115

Fingertip Freedom 118

INTRODUCTION

Each time we put stitches on needles we begin a new journey, and so it has been with this book. An evening or weekend's worth of engagement and pleasurable escape comes with every project, along with a challenge or two to hold your interest. But no matter where you go with your knitting, rest assured that the finish-line will never be very far from the starting point. Sometimes life calls for a quick yarn fix. A little ball of softness calls and we can't wait an entire sweater's length of time to see the results. Hence this book.

A lot of love went into this collection of warm bits and arm candy—hats, scarves, gloves and mittens, sweaters for our doggie friends, plus a delicious evening bag. I honed my glove-making techniques on my husband's bear claws. My next-door neighbor's dog, Hamish, an adventuresome Yorkshire, and his dog friend, the congenial Buddy, who leads a happily pampered life by the New England shore, both agreed to serve as my pattern models for the woof warmers. Each inspired a dog sweater in this collection, one drawing from the Fair Isle and intarsiate techniques and the other from the Aran tradition. However, in the end they were photographed on a well-behaved and intelligent Jack Russell. He seemed very happy to wear them. (He was being bribed at the time with tidbits of food!)

Our canine friends are definitely among the "knitworthy," a term I heard recently from a knitter to describe those who truly appreciate the love that comes with a handcrafted item. The designation also clearly fits my sister-in-law, who periodically continues to enthuse over very simple sweaters I knitted for her

twins three seasons ago. The twins' arrival surprised both my 40-something sister-in-law and her husband less than two years ago. As I thought of this couple, spending their days following the peripatetic movements of their toddlers, the image of a zigzag race course came to mind. The zig-zag worked its way into a brightly colored child's hat that I'm sharing with you.

As for myself, I have always been a scarf girl, from the time I accompanied my mother to Paris in the late Sixties. I couldn't be more delighted that scarves are back in a big way. They're not only neck warmers but style statements. With the right pattern, color, and texture, the scarf makes an ensemble out of disparate clothes. Knitting a scarf need not bring on boredom. It can be the perfect showplace for your most intriguing stitches: lace, cables and bobbles, color, or short rows. All of these options, and more, come with the scarves on the pages ahead in this book.

I've learned a great deal working on all the little bits of pleasure in this book, and I present them to you with the hope that they will also reward you with delight, both in the making experience and in the final product. Each project has its own revelations. For me, the biggest surprise was the fun I had making gloves and a pair of flip-top mittens with half-fingers. For one thing, I loved seeing the knitting grow around the hands each time my designated model tried them on. By the end of each pair, I was left in renewed awe of the versatility of the human hand. On a more technical level, I discovered that the type of needles made all the difference in covering up those fingers and thumbs. Made of bamboo as light as air, they have a surface tension that holds those slippery stitches in place, no matter what.

Some people are put off by the stop-and-go aspect of working gloves. You are always breaking off yarn in one place and starting it in a new place, and putting some number of stitches on a holder while you work on just a few. But try forgetting about the whole glove and think only about the step in process. One finger of a glove can be yours in about a half hour's time, or several 15 minute segments spent waiting for the school bus or sitting in the doctor's office. How many short blocks of good knitting time slip by us in a week? Probably a glove's worth do.

Knitting is perfect for managing time instead of letting it manage you. The projects in this collection can go anywhere with you. In addition to giving you that quick yarn fix, your needles and string will take you in new directions as you expand your experience and confidence. Even a novice knitter is ready for the felted cloche, bag, and scarf that are offered here. Part of the magic of felting is that it erases any irregularity in your stitches, making it a perfect way to pursue the quest for even tension, an elusive goal for me for many years, I might add. There are diagrams to help you understand some of the techniques involved, and several tips scattered throughout the projects to make things easy.

Just try one new thing at a time. I hope you have just as much fun knitting from this book as I had creating it!

GINA MACRIS

SOME
TECHNIQUES
& STITCHES

In this chapter you will find detailed explanations of various
knitting techniques and stitches you will find as you work your
way through the book's projects.

Some Techniques & Stitches

To a knitter, there is infinite possibility in two needles and a ball of yarn. Many times knitters realize that possibility revolves around the details of the knitting. Different techniques play starring roles, depending on the project.

In a scarf, it may be a provisional cast-on that allows knitting from the center out to each end. In a sea of stockinette stitch, the critical element may be the way a stitch increase disappears into the fabric. Sometimes embellishment may be the outstanding feature, like a fringe made of twisted cord.

Gaining expertise in various techniques expands our competence as knitters, builds confidence, and increases the chances of pleasing results.

On the following pages you can find details of some of the techniques that went into the interesting designs appearing in this book.

PROVISIONAL CAST-ON

Provisional cast-ons are used when the design calls for stitches to be picked up after one section of knitting, as for the lacy scarf on page 80. The methods illustrated below and opposite use scrap yarn and knitting needles. When it is time to pick up the stitches, unravel the waste yarn slowly, releasing one live stitch and picking it up with a needle before unraveling the next stitch. If the yarn resists, cut it carefully. If you fall short of the number of stitches required, examine the pick-up line, particularly the edges, for missed stitches. If you can't find any, add one or more at the edges to get the required number.

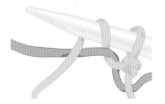

1 With your working yarn make a loose slip knot and place it on a knitting needle. To ensure that there will be enough slack in the yarn to accommodate the stitches picked up later, use a needle three sizes larger than the size the directions specify.

2 Hold the waste yarn next to the base of the slip knot and pass the working yarn under it. Bring the working yarn forward (wrapping it around the waste yarn), then passing the working yarn over the top of the needle from front to back. From the back, bring the working yarn forward, passing it in front of (over) the waste yarn.

3 Repeat Step 2 until all the desired stitches are cast on, with the waste yarn caught in each stitch. Switch to the proper-sized needles when you begin knitting.

CROCHETED CHAIN & CAST-ON

1 Using a crochet hook, make a slip knot and place it onto the crochet hook. Ths is the start of a crochet chain that will have twice the number of stitches you want to cast on.

2 Pass the working yarn from back to front over the shaft of the hook and to the back again under the hook, then with the yarn hooked at the tip, draw the yarn through the existing loop on the hook to make the first chain stitch. Repeat this motion for as many stitches as needed.

3 Put the chain face down, so that the side which looks like a braid is away from you and the bumps in the back show. Insert a knitting needle in the back of the second-to-last loop in the crochet chain, pick up and knit one stitch. Repeat this process in every other loop of the chain until the desired number of stitches are cast on.

BACKWARD LOOP CAST-ON

This method is not so sturdy as many of the other methods. I prefer this loop in felted items because it makes a crisper edge than the thicker methods.

The thin edge of the backward loop also works well in gloves, where stitches must be cast on in the crevices between the fingers.

1 Make a slip knot and place it on a knitting needle. The working yarn, coming from the ball, wraps around the front of the left thumb to the back. Hold the yarn down in the palm of your left hand.

2 Rotate your thumb toward the needle to make a closed loop, and insert the needle from front to back (bottom to top) into the loop.

3 Slip the loop off your thumb onto the needle, and pull the working yarn to tighten the loop. Repeat the thumb-wrapping and loop-transfer for the desired number of stitches.

INCREASES

The lifted increase results in a nearly invisible added stitch to your knitting. There are two methods for working it, depending on where the increase is to be inserted. See the illustrations to the right, and the two below.

Increase from the right:

1 Insert the right needle from front to back in the side of the stitch on the row below the next stitch on the left needle, drawing up a loop.

2 Knit a new stitch in this loop, working it onto the right needle. Then knit the stitch above (the next stitch on the left needle) to continue work.

Increase from the left:

1 Insert the tip of the left needle from back to front into the side of the loop in the second row below the first stitch on the right needle.

Make 1 (M1) is another useful and nearly invisible increase. The new stitch is created from the horizontal strand between two existing stitches. See the two illustrations below and the two on the opposite page under the heading: To slant to the right.

Make 1: To slant to the left:

2 Knit a new stitch in this loop. (If you insert the left needle into the row directly below the knitted stitch on the right needle to knit the new stitch, it will just unravel.

1 Insert the tip of the left needle from front to back under the horizontal connecting strand between the stitch just knitted and the next stitch on the left needle.

2 Knit a stitch through the back of the loop, twisting it to the left in the process.

SPECIAL DECREASES

SSK Sometimes it is desirable to get a decrease that slants to the left, without any twisted stitches. SSK does the trick.

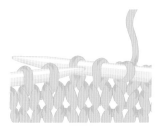

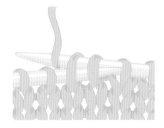

1 One at a time, slip two stitches knitwise from the left needle to the right needle.

2 Insert the left needle from left to right through the front loops of the two slipped stitches, then knit them together.

Make 1: To slant to the right:

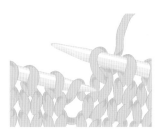

1 Insert the tip of the left needle from back to front under the horizontal connecting strand between the stitch just knitted and the next one on the left needle, lifting the strand onto the left needle.

2 Knit a stitch through the front of the loop, twisting it to the right in the process.

Double vertical decrease

1 Insert the right needle knitwise in the second stitch, then the first st on the left needle and slip these first two stitches onto the right needle.

2 Knit the next stitch on the left needle and pass the two slipped stitches over it. Two stitches are decreased.

Triple vertical decrease
Follow the procedure for the double vertical decrease, but instead of knitting one stitch before passing over the two slipped stitches, knit two stitches together. Three stitches are decreased.

FAIR ISLE

Fair Isle is a real location—one of the Shetland Islands off the northern coast of Scotland. "Fair Isle" has lent its name to a particular style of knitting originating here, popularized by the English upper classes in the early 1900s.

Fair Isle knitting mixes many colors in intricate geometric patterns, traditionally with no more than two colors used on any one row and those colors interchanged every few stitches, making the color patterns easy to work. Today, the term "Fair Isle" is used to describe colored patterns in general, regardless of the particular pattern or its origin.

The Fair Isle technique, worked in stockinette stitch, uses only two colors at a time, with frequent changes between them. At any given point there is one working strand and another carried in the back of the knitting. The most critical aspect of Fair Isle knitting is to carry the color not in use loosely across the back of the work until it is needed again, so that it does not pull the other-colored stitches just worked together into a pucker when the colors switch places. Work loosely, but not too loosely or the stitches themselves will end up too loosely made. With a little practice, you will learn to get it just right.

If you haven't tried Fair Isle knitting before, practice this technique with scrap yarn before taking on a project. Once you settle on a project, remember to begin with a swatch in the specified color pattern because the stranding of one yarn behind another can affect gauge.

The yarn not in use is always carried on the wrong side of the work, on the back for knit rows and on the front for purl rows. There are various ways to carry

along the non-working yarn, depending on the intervals between color changes, using one or both hands to hold the yarn. Two-handed stranding goes faster, but you must be familiar with the nuances of holding the yarn in both the left hand (continental style) and the right hand (usual American style) as you work. If the intervals between color changes are one to four stitches, the alternating yarns may simply be picked up, one after another, going over or under the previously worked strands. If the intervals are longer, the carried yarn must be woven in or twisted around the working yarn so it does not sag on the back and adversely affect the tension.

All this weaving and twisting and carrying-along is sure to wind the two colors around each other in a long column of tangles unless precautions are taken. The simplest way to minimize tangling the yarn at color changes is to remember to carry one color over the dropped yarn and the other color under the dropped yarn. To control the length of the tail between the knitting and the ball of yarn, close up the ball in a zippered bag. Check the yarn frequently and untwist as you go.

If there is just a touch of one color in your project, you can wind the needed yarn on a bobbin. Alternatively, if the project calls for many colors, cut off yard-long lengths of yarn as you need them and weave in the beginnings and ends.

CORRECT AND INCORRECT TENSION

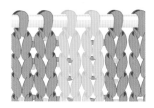 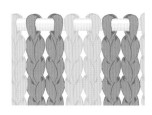 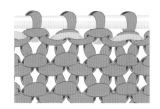 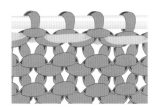

1 Correct tension on the right side. Stitches are relaxed.

2 Tension that is too tight, viewed from the right side. Stitches pucker.

3 Correct weaving on the wrong side.

4 Incorrect weaving on the wrong side.

HOLDING THE YARN WITH ONE HAND
On the knit side:

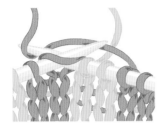 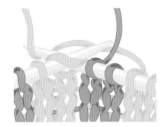

1 Drop the first yarn and pick up the second one, passing it over the first yarn. Work to the next color change.

2 At the next color change, drop the second yarn and pick up the first yarn, passing it under the second yarn. Work to the next color change.

On the purl side

1 Drop the first yarn and pick up the second one, passing it over the first yarn. Work to the next color change.

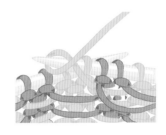

2 At the next color change, drop the second yarn and pick up the first yarn, passing it under the second yarn and begin work.

HOLDING THE YARN WITH BOTH HANDS
On the knit side

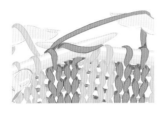 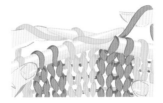

1 Hold the working yarn in the right hand and the waiting (carried) yarn in the left hand. With your right hand, pass the working yarn over the waiting yarn and work to the next color change.

2 At the next color change, the left-hand yarn is the working yarn and the right-hand strand is the waiting yarn. With the left hand, pass the working yarn under the waiting yarn and work, continental style, to the next color change.

On the purl side

1 Hold the working yarn in the right hand and the waiting yarn in the left hand. With your right hand, pass the working yarn over the waiting yarn and work to the next color change.

2 At the next color change, the left hand yarn is the working yarn; the right-hand strand is the waiting yarn. With the left hand, pass the working yarn under the waiting yarn and work, continental style, to the next color change.

To twist strands on the wrong side of the work (when yarn is carried for more than four stitches)

1 On the knit side, twist the working yarn and the carried yarn around each other in back of the work and continue knitting with the same working yarn.

2 On the purl side, twist the working yarn and the waiting yarn around each other in front of you and continue purling with the same working yarn.

WEAVING IN ENDS AS YOU KNIT

In general, it is a good idea to start a new ball of yarn at the beginning of a row, but sometimes that's not possible, especially in color work. When you have loose yarn ends or tails from attaching new yarn, you can work the ends into your knitting to avoid tedious finishing later. When weaving in ends in color work, you will be managing three yarns at this point: the working yarn, the carried (waiting) yarn, and the yarn tail that is being woven in.

Try to anticipate a color change by starting to weave in the beginning tail of a new color at least three or four stitches before it is needed. Similarly, weave in the old color tail for at least three or four stitches after it is last needed.

Where there is great contrast between the colors of the yarn tail and the background against which it is woven, work with care so the contrasting color does not show through on the right side of your work. In some cases, it will be difficult to weave in a tail discreetly while you are knitting. In this case, wait until the knitting is completed, then thread the tail into a tapestry needle and weave it in on the back of the work.

Sometimes it is possible to weave in the tail of the new yarn against itself. This works well at the beginning of a row or in the middle of a row.

To weave in a tail while working on the knit side

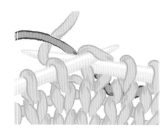

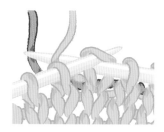

1 Hold yarn tail to be woven in the left hand and pass it over the right needle. Knit the next stitch with the working yarn, which passes under the woven yarn tail.

2 Drop the waiting yarn and knit the next stitch with the working yarn, which passes over the woven yarn tail. Pick up the yarn tail and return to Step 1. Repeat Steps 1 and 2 for several stitches.

To weave in a tail while working on the purl side

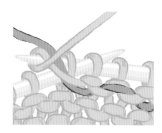

1 Pass the yarn tail to be woven over the right needle. Purl the next stitch with the working yarn, which passes under the woven tail yarn.

2 Drop the waiting yarn, and purl the next stitch with the working yarn, which passes over the woven yarn tail. Pick up the yarn tail and return to Step 1. Repeat Steps 1 and 2 for several stitches.

INTARSIA

*Intarsia is color work in which a separate strand of yarn is used for each
section of color, rather than carrying the non-working yarns across the whole
row as you do in Fair Isle knitting.*

For intarsia, the yarns are interlocked when the colors are changed to prevent holes in the work. Depending on the number of colors used and the amount needed for each, separate colors may be used wound around bobbins. Or, for small areas, simply cut lengths of one to two yards, letting the strands hang loose on the wrong side when they are not being worked.

The different-colored strands must be twisted around each other on every row when the colors change on a vertical line. When the color change runs diagonally, the two stands can be twisted every other row. They are twisted on knit rows when the color change slants to the right, and twisted on purl rows when the line slants to the left.

VERTICAL LINE

CHANGING COLORS ON THE DIAGONAL
Right-slanting diagonal   Left-slanting diagonal

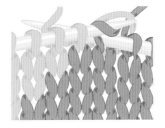

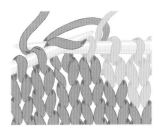

1 At a vertical color change on a knit row, drop the old color on wrong side of work (on the back for knit rows), and pick up the new color from under the old color. The new color then passes over the old to begin knitting the next stitch.

1 On a knit (right-side) row, the diagonal slants to the right. To twist colors, drop the old color to the wrong side, bring the new to the right, passing it up and over the old color, to begin the first stitch of the new color block.

1 On a knit (or right side) row, the diagonal slants to the left. Without twisting, pick up the new color from under the old color and begin knitting the next color block.

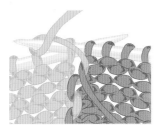

2 At a vertical color change on a purl row, drop the old color on wrong side of work (in the front on purl rows) and pick up the new color from under the old color. The new color now passes over the old to begin purling the next stitch.

2 On a purl-side row, this same diagonal slants to the left. Drop the old color. Pick up the new color from under the old color and begin to purl in the new color block without twisting.

2 On a purl-side row, this same diagonal slants to the right. To twist colors on a purl row, drop the old color. Pick up the new color from under the old color, passing it up and over the old color, wrapping around it, to purl the first stitch in the new color block.

CABLING

Cabling is shorthand for marvelous texture. This term covers all manner of stitches switching places with each other over the surface of the knitted fabric.

The stitches may move either to the right or the left. If they move to the right, the stitches they replace are put on a cable needle and held in back until the transition is made. Then the stitches on the cable needle are knitted back into the fabric. If the stitches are to move to the left, they are held on a cable needle in front of the work while replacement stitches are worked in their stead. Then the left-moving stitches are knitted off the cable needle into their new location. These principles work whether one or more stitches are trading places. The illustrations on this page explain the moves in detail.

MAKE A RIGHT (BACK) CABLE

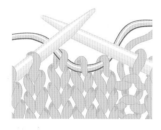

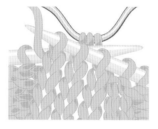

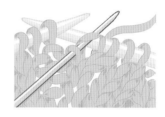

1 Put one or more stitches onto a cable needle and hold them in back of the work.

2 Pulling the yarn tightly to avoid a gap, knit the remaining stitches of the cable

3 Knit the stitches from the cable needle.

MAKE A LEFT (FRONT) CABLE

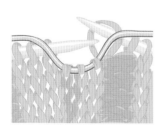

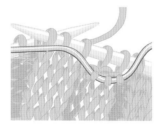

1 Put one or more stitches onto a cable needle and hold them in front of the work.

2 Pulling the yarn tightly to avoid a gap, knit the remaining stitches of the cable.

3 Knit the stitches from the cable needle. To prevent the last stitch of the cable—the one now on the left edge—from becoming loose, tug the yarn tightly before beginning the next stitch.

TWISTED CORD

One or more strands can be twisted, but to set the twist, the cord must be doubled back on itself.

1 Start with strands that are three times the desired finished length. Knot them at each end. Insert a pencil or knitting needle in each secured end and twist. Ideally, someone else can hold one end of the cord while you twist the other end. If no one is available to help, loop one or more strands over a doorknob at one end, with the distance between the knob and the knot about three times the desired finished length.

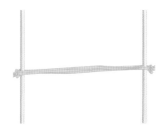

2 Twist one end of the cord until it starts to kink.

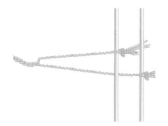

3 Stop twisting. Without losing any twist, fold the cord in half, bringing the two ends together. The two halves of the cord will wind around each other. Tie knots at each end, leaving 1" (2.5cm) tails that can be unraveled into tassels.

I-CORD

I-cord is a seamless narrow tube with great versatility in embellishment. It requires two double-pointed (dp) needles or a short circular needle.

Instructions

Cast on several stitches, usually 3 to 5. Hold the dp needle (or point of circular needle) with the stitches in your left hand. Knit the stitches, *slide the stitches to the opposite end of the needle. Place this needle (or point of circular needle) with the stitches in the left hand. Drawing the working yarn firmly across the back of the knitted stitches, knit the stitches again. Repeat from * to make the cord to the desired length. Knit 3 stitches together then fasten off.

FRINGE

Cut yarn strands twice the length desired for the finished fringe, plus a little extra for knotting. For each fringe, fold the strand (or strands) in half. With a crochet hook, draw the folded end from front to back through the edge being fringed, forming a small loop.

Draw the cut ends of the strand through the loop and pull gently on them to tighten the knot. Trim the fringe ends even.

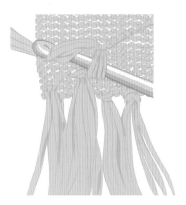

KNITTING IN THE ROUND

When you have cast on the desired number of stitches, be certain that the stitches are not twisted around the needle before you join them. If they are twisted, then the process might take longer and not look correct.

To make a smooth transition between cast-on stitches and the first round, cast on one more stitch than specified in the instructions, and place this extra stitch on the left needle. Knit this stitch together with the next stitch on the left needle.

To keep track of the number of rounds as you work, place a marker between the first and last stitches, slipping it from left to right point of the circular needle as you work each round.

To avoid "ladders," or loose joins when using double-pointed needles, don't switch needles at the same place on every round. Instead, stagger the transitions. After working all the stitches from the left-hand needle, you normally transfer it to the right hand to become the working needle. Before you take this step, however, knit one of two additional stitches from the next needle in line. This way, if the join between the two needles is not quite tight enough, it will show less.

One advantage of knitting in the round for stockinette stitch is that it eliminates the need for purling. Because many of us knit and purl at slightly different tensions, eliminating purl rows in the project means they must be eliminated in the swatch to get the correct gauge. This can be done without actually knitting in the round, although it requires two double-pointed needles or a circular needle. At the end of every knit row, simply carry the yarn loosely across the back of the work and start knitting again at the start with another RS row. That's all there is to it.

Left
Knitting in the round makes it easier to create the patterns in a project such as this multicolored children's hat.

GRAFTING

For an invisible joining between two rows of unbound-off stitches lined up head to head, grafting is well worth the effort. Grafting, or Kitchener stitch, helps finish off the convertible mittens on page 118.

Knitters also often use grafting to joint stitches at the toes of knitted socks to make a comfortable seamless joining, so it is a useful technique to learn.

The illustrations, for clarity, do not show any knitting needles, but in reality, all but one or two stitches in waiting should be kept on needles, one for each piece to be grafted, while you join the pieces. Don't release the loops from the needle until you are ready to weave them together. Use a tapestry needle and a length of yarn that matches the pieces to be joined. Remember that the needle goes through each stitch twice: once purlwise and once knitwise.

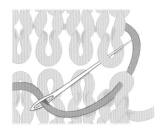

1 Working from right to left, insert the tapestry needle purlwise through the first stitch on the bottom and then knitwise through the first stitch on the top. Draw the yarn through.

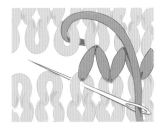

2 Return your attention to the stitch on the bottom, inserting the needle knitwise.

3 You may pull the yarn through at this point, or in an extension of the previous motion, simply insert the needle purlwise through the loop immediately to the left of the one just worked.

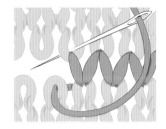

4 Go back to the top loop that has just one strand of yarn worked through it. Insert the needle purlwise in this loop.

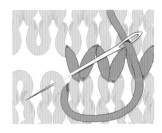

5 At this point you may draw the yarn through, or continuing the previous motion, insert the needle knitwise into the stitch to the left of the stitch just worked above, drawing the yarn through.

Repeat steps 2 through 5 across.

Short Rows

Short rows add another dimension to your knitting, allowing you to transform it from a flat surface into a gently curved piece. Only a portion of the stitches already on the needles is used for working the short rows.

These are the "live" stitches that are worked back and forth while the other stitches remain idle as the short rows are worked. To shape the piece gradually, the short rows of active stitches may lengthen or shorten, according to the specific directions, so that idle stitches may become "live," or previously "live" stitches may become idle on later rows. The directions for your project will guide you in this process.

To prevent holes in stockinette stitch, a slipped stitch at the turning point of each short row is wrapped in a special way. This also allows the demarcation between the short row stitches and the idle stitches to be less obvious when you resume knitting across all the stitches once again. Garter stitch does not require this wrapping technique.

Simply turn the work at the end of the short row and move the working yarn to the back of the knitting, ready for the next stitch.

Whether the directions indicate wrapping or not, it is wise to use markers to indicate the boundaries of the short rows. This way you do not become confused.

The series of illustrations on the opposite page will make this technique much clearer. Read through the steps carefully, then work in old yarn until you feel at ease with the process. This is a great ne skill, one you will be able to use in all manner of knitted items.

Left
Short rows can create interesting effects as this detail of the scarf project on page 56 reveals.

TO WRAP STITCHES AT END OF SHORT ROWS

On the knit side

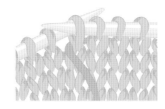

1 With yarn in back, slip the next stitch purlwise.

2 Bring yarn to front of work between the two needles.

3 Pass slipped stitch back onto left needle. Turn work to purl side and bring yarn to front of row, in position for the first purl stitch.

On the purl side

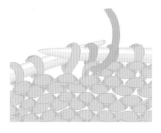

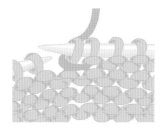

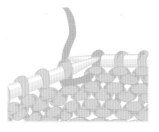

1 With yarn in front, slip the next stitch purlwise.

2 Pass yarn to back of work between the two needles.

3 Return slipped stitch to left needle. Turn work to knit side and bring yarn to back, for knit stitch.

When the short rows have been completed, the bumps created by the wraps must be hidden. See illustrations below.

On the knit side

On the purl side

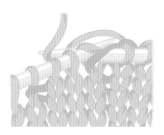

4 Work up to the wrapped stitch. Insert tip of right needle under the wrap and through front of knit stitch. Knit them together and continue until the next wrapped stitch or end of row.

5 Work up to the wrapped stitch. From the back, insert tip of right needle under wrap and lift it onto the left needle. Purl wrap and next stitch on left needle together.

YARN OVERS

The versatile yarn over is at the core of all lace and open-work knitting. For a yarn over, the working yarn wraps around the shaft of the needles, making an extra loop on the needle without working a usual stitch and intentionally creating a hole or eyelet in the knitting.

Lace has elegant symmetry. Each yarn over creates an added stitch (an increase) that is matched at some point by a decrease to maintain an even stitch count. Many times the decreases come immediately after the yarn over on the same row. Sometimes it does not. In the ruffled lace at the wrist of the vintage arm warmers on page 86, for example, all the increases fall on one row, but the balancing decreases are not made until the following row.

There are exceptions to the one increase, one decrease rule, as in the lacy leaf scarf on page 80. Here, the undulating borders are created by increasing and decreasing the total number of stitches over a span of 20 rows. When the pattern calls for yarn over increases without balancing decreases, the stitch count climbs. When yarn over increases are accompanied by double decreases, the stitch count drops.

Having an overview of a pattern makes for more pleasurable knitting, especially with lace. It's like having a sense of the forest while you are focused on the trees. Take time to familiarize yourself with the flow of a lace pattern before you begin. When mistakes happen, as they sometimes do, you'll have a better idea of a way out. If the error is not noticeable, you may be able to correct it with a judiciously placed increase or decrease and move on.

Markers are another way of keeping track of your place in the pattern, and helping to spot a mistake readily. Place a marker between pattern repeats.

How to create a yarn over
1 Between two knit stitches, bring the yarn forward between the knitting needles and pass it over the the top of the right needle to the back.
2 Between two purl stitches, pass the yarn over the right needle to the back and bring it under the right needle to the front again.

> **TIP**
>
> On Abbreviations:
>
> YRN (yarn round needle), YFRN (yarn forward and round needle), YON (yarn over needle) or YFON (yarn forward and over needle) all basically mean YO.
> Sometimes these different names are used to differentiate between YOs that occur between two knit stitches or between a knit and a purl stitch.

Opposite page
Using yarn overs creates a lacy pattern which can be effective in a scarf. Here, soft black yarn is evocative of romantic evenings.

ALL ABOUT FELTING

The felting process transforms loose knitting into a dense fabric virtually impervious to the elements and to frequent wearing. Anyone who's ever tried it, from novice to expert knitter, will tell you it's easy and fun. What more could we want from our knitting experience?

Felting relies on heat, moisture, and friction to raise the microscopic scales on animal hair and interlock them, diffusing the outline of individual stitches in a soft halo of thick fuzz. Sheep's wool, alpaca, and mohair are the most common materials used for felting, although any animal hair will do. There are a few exceptions, however. First, superwash wool, while fabulous for easy-care children's things that can go through the wash, will not felt. This wool is specially treated to resist felting. Second, white and light colors generally will not felt, even if the yarn is all wool, because of bleach or other treatment used to achieve the light color.

A novelty yarn made partly of wool will felt, so long as it is untreated, as will a felting yarn used alongside a synthetic yarn. The best results come from pairings that include a strong eyelash or other such eye-catching component that won't get completely submerged in fuzz.

The only way to know which combinations will be successful is to experiment with some samples.

Before beginning your project, always make a swatch with the specified yarns you plan to use for felting and felt the swatch to test the results on your particular yarns. Work as follows:

Knit the swatch using the yarn and needles specified in the instructions. In general, felting calls for needles about two sizes larger than otherwise recommended. Record the number of stitches and rows in your swatch and measure it for length and width. If pattern instructions give a felted gauge, for example, of 12 stitches and 20 rows over 4" (10cm) square, mark off 12 stitches and 20 rows on your sample before it is felted. Use thread or yarn that does not felt and will be clearly visible after the process is done. Because felting shrinks the knitting considerably, start out with a larger-than-usual sample, about 8" or 9" (20cm or 22cm) square.

The loop cast-on, one rarely used in conventional knitting, is excellent for rendering crisp felted edges. When you change colors as you knit, for the stripes on the hat on page 42, for example, it is far better to cut the yarn ends and weave them into the knitting before felting than to twist them around each other on the inside of the hat after felting, which can leave a noticeable ridge in the felted fabric.

There is more than one method of felting, or fulling, but most knitters use a top-loading washing machine. Put the water level on the lowest setting and turn the temperature dial to hot. Add a drop or two of dish detergent or rinse-free wool wash. Combined with the hot water, the detergent or wool wash will help loosen the individual fibers so they become more amenable to interlocking with their neighbors.

Before putting the item to be felted in the hot water, enclose it in a zippered pillow protector or a knotted pillow case. This is a very important step, because the case prevents the lint shed in the felting process from clogging the washing machine pump.

Set the washing machine for heavy agitation and check the felting process at five-minute intervals for

> **TIP**
>
> Even when the yarn ball says 100 percent wool, the yarn sometimes appears as if it will never felt. It will, but much slower than you would like. If you're not making progress in the washing machine, put your sample in a metal or heat-proof glass bowl and pour boiling water over and soak it overnight. The time spent soaking will loosen the fibers and make them more receptive to agitation.

starters and more often as felting nears completion. When is that? If you've marked the boundaries of a section in your sample that is to shrink to 4" (10cm) square, you're done when you've achieved that measurement. Otherwise, you're done when you can no longer see the stitches and you like what you see.

To increase agitation and speed up the felting process, add a pair or two of old (but clean) jeans, or even a flip-flop or old sneaker. Increasing agitation is especially important when you are felting a small item and can't control the level of water in the washing machine. Be warned that the length of time needed for felting does not conform to a predictable formula. It depends on the yarn, the size of the object—the larger it is the faster it felts—and the amount of water in the washing machine. Felting may take five or ten minutes or an hour. The closer you feel you are to the finish line, the more frequently you should check your project. You can always felt a little more, but if a hat, for example, has shrunk to the point where it will no longer fit you, you'll have to start all over again, or give it away.

Never let the washing machine run through a rinse and spin cycle with your felted item inside. The spin cycle can create permanent, unwanted creases that will ruin all your hard work. When you're finished with

Above
Felting gives a firm shape to a hat such as the one shown here.

agitation, remove the felted item from the washing machine and rinse it in plain running water, unless you used a rinse-free wool wash. If you do that, then no rinsing is necessary.

Sometimes during felting, two or more layers of a project stick together. Just pull them apart on one of your periodic checks inside the zippered pillow protector. When the shapes of pieces get distorted, for example, rectangles become trapezoids, don't hesitate to pull them back into shape before putting them back in the washing machine. After two or three such treatments, your felting will get the message.

For a finished look after the felting is done, block your project. Blot out excess moisture by rolling it up in a towel. Tug it, pull it, and pin it down on a blocking board, if necessary, to achieve the proper shape. To block a hat, pull it over a ball or an overturned bowl that is the circumference of the wearer's head. Once the shape and the dimensions are set, allow the project to dry completely. The blocking process must be repeated each time the finished project is washed.

EMBELLISHMENTS

Such a lovely word—embellishments! Imagine the glamorous projects that
you will be able to create with your talent for embellishing something plain.
Yarn will take on a new persona; it will gleam and shine, light will dance
off the fibers as it catches a glimpse of a bead, a sequin, or a pearl.

An embellishment means not only textured stitches and fancy borders such as lace and other fine sheer fabrics, but beads, sequins, feathers, buttons and ribbons. Even embroidery and appliqué can be a trim.

Realizing some of these possibilities is a matter of being willing to have an adventure in style. Wherever I go, I love to look around and note the details of the way a landscape presents so many different shades of green and brown, or the interesting ways people dress on the street. These images are filed away in my mind, to be retrieved, hopefully, at the exact moment when a design needs just something extra.

It is best to make design choices before the knitting ever begins. For example, if you want to run a ribbon through knitted fabric, you must place an opening at strategic locations. First determine where you want the ribbon to go in and out of the fabric. At each point, just add a yarn-over, followed immediately by a decrease, so that the stitch count remains the same. Your strategically placed holes can run vertically, horizontally, or diagonally, depending on your desires.

The ladder effect on the cuff of the bright red gloves on page 111 got a lot of attention on the occasions it was knit in public and the small pearls were an excellent choice as an embellishment, adding another level of chic style to the gloves.

I recently saw plain gloves embellished with a row of heart-shaped buttons at the wrist in the same color as the yarn. The effect was charming. Embroidery on the back of the hand, a ruffle at the cuff, or a row of strategically-placed yarn-overs to hold a ribbon running around the wrist, are other decorative choices.

Ruffles are fabulous for a feminine touch. Basic ruffles are easy. Double or triple the number of stitches specified in the cast-on edge, depending on how much wave you want. These soft embellishments can go around the brim of a hat, around collars, hems, the bottom of sleeves, baby blankets, anywhere an

Left
Buttons always add character to a piece of knitted work. Here, buttons made from natural shell are just waiting for a cream-colored cardigan.

attractive edging is required. They can be of the same color, or a different color, patterned or plain. Think about the many ways to add style with a ruffle and work it into a design as an experiment.

Bobbles are examples of knitted appliqué that can be added directly to the fabric after the main body of a knitted project is complete. They can be contrasting colored "polka dots" on a plain background, or they can march around a hat brim or a sleeve cuff in a contrasting (or matching) band.

Feathers, soft and delicate, can be added to anything. Sewn along a border as a trim to a delicate shoulder cape, or added in a group to the wrist of a sweater (maybe tied with a length of ribbon), they will be very impressive.

These ideas are intended to fuel your creativity as you build confidence both in your knitting and your sense of style. You might not have a penchant for sequins, or feathers, but some divine trim will catch your eye and you will suddenly see it as part of your next knitting project!

From top right
Tiny fabric rosebuds and subtle velvet ribbons can enrich any knitted design. A strip of sequins is easy to add to a garment.

COLOR AND YARN

Color is a powerful force in our lives. It is no trivial thing to select a color you will live with for a long time, especially if it involves a costly yarn and many hours at the needles. Following is some advice on choosing colors.

I love color. If you're selecting one color, there is nothing wrong with just picking what you like. Some people know intuitively which colors look good on them; however, when the seasons change and the fashion statements are in all of the magazines, then it is time to indulge in a little color therapy and look at color in a different way.

There is a scientific basis for color harmony that depends on the way the human eye registers the various hues. The perception varies, depending on the relative placement of each color. Color combinations have a logic that is codified in the color wheel. Pocket-sized color wheels are yours for a few dollars.

The color wheel is built on three essential colors: red, yellow, and blue, the primary colors that form all other colors. When they are mixed together, they create three secondary colors: orange, green, and violet (purple). Beyond orange, green and violet are the six tertiary colors, which are made by mixing one primary color and one secondary color. Analogous colors (colors adjacent each other on the wheel) are the colors to concentrate on if you are nervous about color because they combine more successfully.

If you want lots of color and want to make safe choices at the same time, let someone else do all the work and pick a self-striping, or variegated yarn. Multicolored yarns are so ubiquitous, available in every gauge and weight. Even cable and lace patterns will be successful when made with variegated yarns, as long as the shifts in color are subtle enough so as not to detract from the stitch patterns—and that is an important rule in knitting.

Below
A soft haze of blue, purple to paler pink reveal a complementary, and calming, color scheme.

Variegated yarns can be used in combination with other yarns. In the two-color brioche stitch scarves (page 62) both versions depend on one multicolored yarn and one solid color. The scarves look different but the color exercise was similar. In each project the scarf starts with the variegated yarn color and works to its companion, picking up one of the existing blues in the first choice. In each case, the companion color had the same value, that is, the same degree of color saturation or lack of it, depending on the amount of whitish tint, toned gray, or shaded black that was mixed with the pure hue.

Among the multi-colored projects in this book, the child's hat uses analogous colors (colors adjacent each other on the wheel), jumping from orange to the red family, where it draws from one darker tone and one tint—a pink.

Colors close to each other combine in a calming effect, while greater distances between them produce a more vibrant result. As an example, try putting navy blue, royal blue and pale blue together and you'll see there is a harmony. High-contrast complementary combinations are the most difficult to pull off; yarns with equal measures of, say, bright blue and bright orange would strain the eyes, to say the least.

Choosing colors to knit with is similar to choosing paint colors. Interior designers always try out a variety of colors before committing an entire wall to one of them. You can do the same to preview any color effect by wrapping each yarn you select twice around an index card. Do this with several color combinations then place the cards a distance away from each other in natural light so you can get the full impact. If you want a sure-fire color exercise, pick a color you like, find a color close to it in the spectrum, and knit the colors in alternating stripes of two rounds each.

Also consider the importance of neutrals, including white, natural, gray and black, as well as colors that can be used as neutrals, such as chocolate brown, navy, tans, and taupe.

There are endless color combinations and sources of color inspiration, from the man-made world and from nature. As an exercise in understanding how color combines, collate files of magazine clippings of clothes and interior accessories you like, plus images that speak to you of color. The more you do this, the better at color you will become.

In working through one combination after another lies the fun of color.

Below
The two variegated yarns have a touch of orange and pale blue, which will bring the cream yarn to life.

THE
PROJECTS

Hats

Be well ahead of the fashion game when you knit and wear one of these warm and colorful hats designed especially with you, or a friend, in mind.

A CHIC CLOCHE

This felted topper, ringed with a band of stripes, is impervious to weather. Its wide rolled brim will keep the snow and rain out of your eyes all winter long.

Skill Level: ■■□□
Materials:
Yarn: MC & CC: Plymouth Galway worsted 210yd (192m)/3.5oz (100g) ball
Color: For MC, color 117
For CC, color 132
Amount: 2 balls MC, 1 ball CC
Total yardage 420yd (384m) for MC, 210yd (192m) for CC
Needles: US 11 (8mm) circular needle 24" (61cm) long
One set US 11 (8mm) double-pointed needles
Gauge: 16sts and 31 rows = 4" (10cm) after felting.
Finished Size: Average adult head: 21" to 23" (53.3cm to 58.4cm)

INSTRUCTIONS

Using MC, cast on 124 sts.
Rounds 1 to 3: Knit.
Round 4: Decrease 6 sts evenly spaced. (118 sts)
Rounds 5-9: Knit
Round 10: Knit, decreasing 6 sts evenly spaced. (112 sts)
Round 11-15 : Knit.
Round 16: Decrease 6 sts evenly spaced. (106 sts)
Round 17-20: Knit.
Round 21: Knit, decreasing 6 sts evenly spaced. (100 sts)
Round 22-25: Knit.

Round 26: Knit, decreasing 6 sts evenly spaced. (94 sts)
Round 27 to 30: Knit.
Round 31: Knit, decreasing 6 sts evenly spaced. (88 sts)
Round 32: Drop MC, pick up CC. Knit for 3 rounds.
Next round: Drop CC, pick up MC. Knit for 3 rounds.
Next round: Drop MC. Pick up CC. Knit for 3 rounds.
Next round: Drop CC, pick up MC. Knit for 3 rounds.
Next Round: Drop MC Pick up CC. Knit for 3 rounds.
Next round: Drop CC Pick up MC.
Knit even for 16 rounds.

Shape top:
Round 1: *K9, k2 tog, repeat from * to end. (80 sts)
Round 2 and all even-numbered rows: Knit.
Round 3: *K8, k2 tog, repeat from * to end. (72 sts)
Round 5: *K7, k2 tog, repeat from * to end. (64 sts)
Round 7: *K6, k2 tog, repeat from * to end. (56 sts)
Round 9: *K5, k2 tog, repeat from * to end. (48 sts)
Round 11: *K4, k2 tog, repeat from * to end. (40 sts)
Round 13: *K3, k2 tog, repeat from * to end. (32 sts)
Round 15: *K2, k2 tog, repeat from * to end. (24 sts)
Round 17: *K1, k2 tog, repeat from * to end. (16 sts)
Round 19: *K2 tog, repeat from * to end (8 sts.)

Cut yarn and run twice through remaining 8 sts. Felt hat and block according to the felting instructions on page 32.

TIP

When changing colors it is better to cut the yarn
ends and weave them into the knitting before
felting than to twist them around each other on
the inside of the hat after felting, which can leave
a noticeable ridge in the felted fabric.

A CHILD'S COLORFUL CAP

A sunburst of color on this snuggly child's hat will brighten any winter day. Traveling stitches emboss a zig-zag pattern on a field of multicolored stripes.

INSTRUCTIONS

With smaller needles and using color B, cast on 92 (102, 114) sts and work in k2, p2 ribbing for 3 rounds. Drop B and pick up color A. Continue in ribbing for five more rounds, increasing 6 (10, 12) sts evenly spaced on the last round. 98 (112, 126) sts. Ribbing to measure 1½" (4cm) in length. Change to larger needles and begin pattern.

(Rounds 1 to 10, slant to the right)
Round 1: With A, *p5, put next st on cn (cable needle) and hold to back, k 1st st on left needle, k st from cn, k4, put next st on cn and hold to back, k first st on left needle, p st from cable needle, p 1, repeat from * to end of round.

Round 2: and all even- numbered rounds: K the knit stitches and p the purl stitches.

Round 3: *P4, put next st on cn and hold to back, k first st on left needle, k st from cn, k4, put next st on cn and hold to back, k 1st st on left needle, p st from cn, p2, repeat from * to end of round, ending with p1.

Round 5: *P3, put next st on cn and hold to back, k first st on left needle, k st from cn, k4, put next st on cn and hold to back, k first st on left needle, p st from cn, p3, repeat from * to end of round.

Round 6: Drop A and pick up B.

Skill level: ◼◻◻

Materials:

Yarn:	RYC Cashsoft DK 143yd (130m)/1.75oz (50g)
Color:	For Color A: 510 Clementine
	For Color B: 512 Poppy
	For Color C: 506 Crush
Amount:	1 ball each colors A, B, and C
Total Yardage:	143yd (130m) each for colors A, B, and C for all sizes
Needles:	16" (40cm) long circular needles in US sizes 6 (4mm) and 4 (3.5mm) or sizes to get gauge. One set double-pointed needles in US size 6 (4mm) or size to get gauge.
Gauge:	25 sts and 30 rows = 4" x 4" (10cm x 10cm)
Finished sizes:	Approx. 16" (18", 20") [40.5cm (45.7cm, 50.8cm)] circumference

Round 7: *P2,put next st on cn and hold to back, k first st on left needle, k st from cn, k4, put next st on cn and hold to back, k first st on left needle, p st from cn, p4, repeat from * to end of round.

Round 9: *P1, put next st on cn and hold to back, k first st on left needle, k st from cn, k4, put next st on cn and hold to back, k first st on left needle, p st from cn, p5, repeat from * to end of round, ending with p 4.

Round 10: Drop B and pick up C

Rounds 11 to 20, slant to the left:
Round 11: *P1, put next st on cn and hold to front, p first st on left needle, k st from cn, k4, put next st on cn and hold to front, k first st on left needle, k st from cn, p5, repeat from * to end of round.
Round 12: Drop C and pick up B.

Round 13: *P2, put next st on cn and hold to front, p first st on left needle, k st from cn, k4, put next st on cn and hold to front, k first st on left needle, k sts from cn, p4, repeat from * to end of round.

Round 15: *P3, put next st on cn and hold to front, pfirst st on left needle, k st from cn, k4, put next st on cn and hold to front, k first st on left needle, k sts from cn, p3, repeat from * to end of round.

Round 16: Drop B and pick up A.

Round 17: *P4, put next st on cn and hold to front, p first st on left needle, k st from cn, k4, put next st on cn and hold to front, k first st on

left needle, k sts from cn, p2, repeat from * to end of round.

Round 19: *P5, put next st on cn and hold to front, p first st on left needle, k st from cn, k4, put next st on cn and hold to front, k first st on left needle, k st from cn, p1, repeat from * to end of round.

Work even in pattern stitch until piece measures 5½" (6½", 7½") [14cm (16.5cm, 18.5cm)] or desired length.

Crown:
Switch to double-pointed needles when the circumference becomes too small for the circular needle.

Round 1: Dec. 2 (16, 14) sts evenly spaced. (96, 96, 112 sts)
Discontinue stitch pattern but maintain color sequence.
Round 2: *K2, k2tog, repeat from* to end. (72, 72, 84 sts)
Round 3: Work even.
Round 4: *K1, k2tog; repeat from * to end. (48, 48, 56 sts)
Round 5: Work even.
Round 6: *K2tog, repeat from * to end. (24, 24, 28 sts)
Round 7: Repeat round 6. (12, 12, 14 sts)
Round 8: Repeat round 6. (6, 6, 7 sts)

I cord topknot: K2 (2, 3) tog and work I-cord on 5 sts for 4" (10cm).
Fasten off and knot the I-cord.

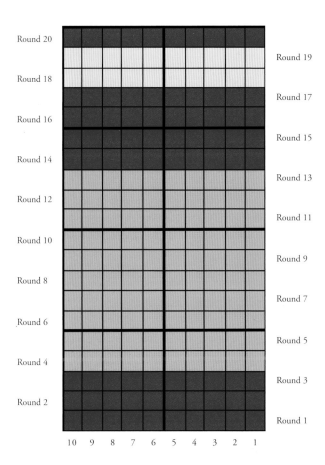

Round 20
Round 19
Round 18
Round 17
Round 16
Round 15
Round 14
Round 13
Round 12
Round 11
Round 10
Round 9
Round 8
Round 7
Round 6
Round 5
Round 4
Round 3
Round 2
Round 1

10   9   8   7   6   5   4   3   2   1

Color sequence for child's hat

Opposite page
Here you can see the pattern of the
ridge as it wends it way down from
the top to the brim.
Right
The top knot is a knotted I-cord
made in one of the three colors.

A SOFT BABY HAT

A ring of bell-shaped ruffles trims an adorable baby hat. This starts out with an impressive number of stitches, but they soon melt away into the scalloped line of the edging. You will love this gift for a newborn.

INSTRUCTIONS

Using the 24" (60cm) circular needle, cast on 224 (238, 266) sts.

Round 1 *p5, k9, repeat from * to end.

Round 2: Repeat round 1.

Round 3: P5, *ssk (slip 2 sts knitwise individually, put left needle through front loops of both stitches, and k them together) k 5, k2 tog. repeat from * to end.

Round 4: *P5, k7, repeat from * to end.

Round 5: *P5, ssk, make double vertical decrease: (sl1k, k2tog, psso) k2tog, repeat from* to end.

Round 6: *P5, k3, repeat from * to end.

Round 7: *P5, k3tog, repeat from * to end.

Round 8: *P5, k1, repeat from * to end. (96, 102, 114) sts.

Repeat Round 8 until piece measures approx. 3" (3½", 4") [7.5cm (9, 10cm)] in length from the beginning of the "stem" that grows out of the bell-shaped ruffle.

Skill level: ■■☐☐
Materials:
Yarn :	Debbie Bliss Baby Cashmerino 136yd (125m)/1.75oz (50g)
Color:	608
Amount:	1 (1, 2) balls
Total yardage:	136yd (136yd, 272yd) [125m (125m, 250m)]
Needles :	US size 5 (3.75mm) circular needle 24" (60cm) long One set double-pointed needles US size 5 (3.75mm) or size to get gauge
Gauge:	25 sts and 32 rows = 4" in ribbed pattern
Sizes:	Birth to 6 months, 6 to 18 months. Circumference: 15" (16½",18½") [38cm (42cm, 47cm)]

Shape crown:

Round 1: *P4, k2tog, repeat from * to end.
Round 2: Work even in pattern as established.
Round 3: *P3, k2tog, repeat from * to end.
Round 4: Work even.
Round 5: *P2, k2tog, repeat from * to end.
Round 6: Work even.
Round 7: *P1, k2tog, repeat from * to end.
Round 8: Work even.
Round 9 *K2tog, repeat from * to end. (16, 17, 19) sts
Round 10: Work even.
Round 11: K2tog, repeat from * to end (for two larger sizes, until 3 sts remain), k3 tog. (8, 8, 9) sts
Round 12: For smaller two sizes, k2tog; repeat from * to end. For largest size, k2tog until 3 sts remain. K3tog.
For all sizes: Work on 4 sts for 2 rounds.
Run yarn through live sts and fasten off.

PERFECT POM-POMS

A couple of pom-poms embellish this lighthearted topknot hat, which gets it shape from cabling at the brim and the crown. A thread of white velvet ribbon around the brim adds a decorative touch, too. Alternating stockinette and seed stitch panels also add interest.

Skill level: ◖■■■▭
Materials:
Yarn: Classic Elite Bazic Wool 65yd (59.5m)/1.75oz (50g)
Color: For MC, 2956 Thistle
For CC: 2916 Natural
Amount: MC, 4 balls
CC: 1 ball
Total yardage: MC, 130 yd (119m); CC, 65yd (59.5m)
Needles: 16" long circular needle US 9 (5.5mm) or size to get gauge
Set of double-pointed needles US 9 (5.5mm) or size to get gauge
Gauge: Critical only at cabling round at the brim of the hat, where 36sts, or 3 pattern repeats = 5" (12cm) stretched. To get gauge, swatch in the round.
Finished size: Head circumference: 20" (22") [51cm (56cm)]
Trim: Velvet ribbon 25" (63cm) long

INSTRUCTIONS

Pattern
Using MC, cast on 120 (132) sts.

Rounds 1, 3, 5, 7: *K6, p1, k1, p1, k1, p1, k1; repeat from * to end.
Rounds 2, 4, 6, 8: K6, *p1, k1, p1, k1, p1, k1; repeat from * to end.
Round 9 (Cabling round): *Place 6 sts on cable needle and place to back of work, p1, k1, p1, k1, p1, k1, k6 from cable needle, repeat from * to end.
Round 10: *K1, p1, k1, p1, k1, p1, k6, repeat from * to end.
Round 11: * P1, k1, p1, k1, p1, k7, repeat from * to end.
Repeat rounds 10 and 11 until piece measures approx 6" (7") [15.25cm (17.8cm)], ending with round 11.

Next Round: *k2tog, k1, p1, k2tog, k2tog, k2, k2tog, repeat from * to end. (80, 88 sts)
Next Round: *K1, p1, k1, p1 k4 repeat from * to end.
Next round: *Place 4 sts on cable needle and hold to back, k4, from cable needle, p1, k1, p1, k1, repeat from * to end.
Work in pattern as established 7 rounds more.
Bind off.

Embellishments:

For brim:

Weave a length of ribbon through the holes created by the cable pattern. Tie a knot and a bow at the back. You could also knit an I-cord to the circumference of your head and run this through instead. Graft the ends to finish the I-cord neatly.

For top of hat:

Using CC, cast on 3 sts in conventional manner. Work I cord for approx. 26" (66cm). Leaving a tail of several inches (centimeters), insert I-cord behind one cable in hole created by the cabling. In the space where the I-cord is visible, create a knot to make it stand between the folds. Continue threading the I-cord in and out of the cables and knotting until you have circled the hat. Tie the I-cord together and attach a pom-pom to each end of the I-cord.

POM-POM INSTRUCTIONS

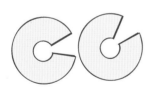

1 Cut two cardboard circles slightly larger than the desired width (or diameter) of the pom-poms, to allow you to trim the edges later. Cut a center hole in the cardboard circles to make a doughnut shape. If desired cut a small slit at the edge to hold the yarn end in place as you wrap.

2 Hold the two circles together and wrap the yarn around them as shown, covering the cardboard with at least 100 wraps. Fill the center circle as completely as possible. Carefully cut the yarn around the edges by angling the scissors between the two cardboard circles. Do not remove the circles yet.

3 Cut a separate length of yarn and slide it between the two circles and tie it tightly to hold the stands together. Now gently remove the circles. Use your finger to fluff the strand ends into a round ball. Trim any uneven ends to make the pom-pom nicely rounded.

SCARVES

A person can never have too many scarves, especially when the cold weather front rushes in. In this chapter, designs with cables, fringes, and textures make each scarf come alive!

A DREAMY SPIRAL SCARF

Grace your neck with this lovely and colorful spiral. Short rows are the key to this long and winding effect, allowing you to work on one to 15 stitches at a time as you build pie-shaped wedges that give this scarf its unusual shape.

Above
Lots and lots of short rows create this spiral fantasy to add style to winter chill.

Skill Level:	◼◼◼▢
Materials:	
Yarn:	Artyarns Supermerino 104yd (95m)/1.75oz (50g) skein
Color:	201
Amount:	2 skeins
Total yardage:	334yd (300m)
Needles:	US 7 (4.5mm) 1 stitch marker
Gauge:	Not necessary
Finished size:	Approx. 60" (152.5cm) long

INSTRUCTIONS

Note: Because this scarf is done entirely in garter stitch, it is not necessary to "wrap" stitches at the end of short rows. For a full discussion of short rows, see page 28.

Special Abbreviations:
pm = place marker
rm = remove marker
Sl1, k1, psso = slip 1 st knitwise, knit one st, pass slipped stitch over

Pattern

Cast on 12 sts.

Row 1: Knit all stitches on needle.

Row 2: Sl1, pm. K11. Turn.

Row 3: Using cable or knit-on method, cast on 1 st (total 13 sts.) Knit to marker (12 live sts), rm. Turn.

Row 4: Sl1, pm, knit 11. Turn.

Row 5: Cast on 1 st (total 14 sts). Knit to marker (12 live sts), rm. Turn.

Row 6: Sl1, pm, knit 11. Turn.

Row 7: Cast on 1 st (total 15 sts.) Knit to marker (12 live sts.), rm. Turn

Row 8: Sl1, pm, knit 11. Turn.

Row 9: Cast on 1 st. (total 16 sts) Knit to marker (12 live sts), rm. Turn.

Row 10: Sl1, place marker, k 11 sts to end. Turn.

Row 11: Cast on 1 (total 17 sts). Knit to marker (12 live sts), rm. Turn.

Row 12: Sl1, place marker, k to end, (11 live sts). Turn.

Row 13 SL1, K1, PSSO, k to marker (10 live sts), rm. Turn.

Row 14: Sl1, pm, k (9 live sts) to end.

Row 15: Sl1, K1, psso, k to marker (8 live sts), rm. Turn.

Row 16: Sl1, pm, k to end (7 live sts)

Row 17: Sl1, K1, psso, k to marker (6 live sts), rm. Turn.

Row 18: Sl1, pm, k to end (5 live sts)

Row 19: Sl1, K1, psso k to marker (4 live sts), rm. Turn.

Row 20: Sl1, pm, k to end (3 live sts). Turn.

Row 21: Sl1, K1, psso, k to marker (2 live sts), rm. Turn.

Row 22: Sl1, k 1. Turn.

Repeat Rows 1 to 22 for pattern.

Work 87 segments in total. Bind off.

Above
Make sure to treat your edge stitches with care for a neat finish to this short row scarf.

Opposite page
Short rows create a spiral shape to this unusual scarf. Casting on and then casting off extra stitches adds a pointed edge for visual interest.

FOCUS ON FRINGE

Fringe with a twist and delicate knots set off this warm winter scarf. It's sure to dress up any ensemble.

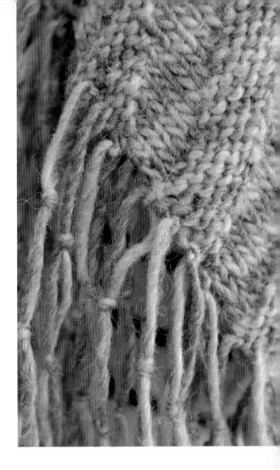

Skill level: ◼◼◻◻
Materials:
Yarn: Mountain Mohair 140yd (128m)/2oz (56g)
Color: For Color A, Daylily
For Color B, Spice
Amount: 2 skeins of each
Total yardage: 280yd (256m) each for A and B
Needles: US size 9 (5.5mm), or size to get gauge
Gauge: 16 st and 24 rows = 4" (10cm)
Finished size: 78" (198cm) long without fringe and 8" (20cm) wide

INSTRUCTIONS

Note: Pattern is repeated in multiples of 12 sts.

With color A, cast on 36 sts.
Row 1: With A, *K6, P6, repeat from * to end.
Row 2: With A, P1, *K6, P6, repeat from * until 11 sts remain. K6, P5. Cut tail about 8" (20cm) long for fringe.
Row 3: Pick up Color B, first leaving an 8" (20cm) tail for fringe. K4, *P6, K6, repeat from * until 8 sts remain. P6, K2.
Row 4: With B, P3, *K6, P6, repeat from * until 9 sts remain. K 6, P3. Cut an 8" (20cm) tail.
Row 5: Pick up A, leaving an 8" (20cm) tail for fringe. K2, *P 6, K 6, repeat from * until 10 sts remain. P6, K4.
Row 6: With A, P5, *K6, P6, repeat from * until 7 sts remain. K6, p1. Cut an 8" (20cm) tail as before.
Row 7: Pick up Color B, leaving an 8" tail for fringe. *P6, K6, repeat from * to end.
Row 8: With B, K1, *P6, k6, repeat from * until

11 sts remain. P6, K 5. Cut an 8" (20cm) tail.
Row 9: Pick up A, leaving an 8" (20cm) tail for fringe. P4, *K6, P6, repeat from* until 8 sts remain. K6, P2.
Row 10: With A, K 3, *P 6, K 6, repeat from * until 9 sts remain. P 6, K3. Leave an 8" (20cm) tail for fringe and cut yarn.
Row 11: Pick up B, leaving an 8" (20cm) tail for fringe. P2, *k6, p6, repeat from * until 10 sts remain. K6, P4.
Row 12: K5, *P 6, K 5, repeat from * until 7 sts remain. P6, K 1. Cut an 8" (20cm) tail.
Repeat rows 1 to 12 for 78" (105cm). Cast off.

Knotted Fringe

Cut strands of fringe to the same length, about 7" (17cm). Using strands in pairs, one of each color, make three knots evenly spaced. Clip ends.

TIP

To ensure the knots are at similar places on the strands, make a single knot around a darning needle. This way, you can 'slide' the knot up and down the strand to the correct position.

BIG IN STYLE

Use two shades of the same yarn for high stitch definition, or push

the boundaries by choosing contrasting textures.

Skill level: ◼◼◼◻

Materials:

Yarn: Rowan Big Wool 87yd (80m)/3.5oz (100g)ball

Color: For Main Color (MC): Shade 21
For Contrasting Color (CC): Shade 33

Amount: 2 balls MC, 2 balls CC

Total Yardage: 174yd (160m) for MC, 174yd (160m) for CC, including fringe

Needles: US 17 (12.75mm)

Gauge: Not necessary

Finished size: Approx 6" (15.25cm) wide and 65" (165cm) long, excluding fringe

Brioche stitch gives a wonderful depth to your knitting—even more so when there are two colors to play with on your needles. This scarf is knitted to exactly the same instructions as the scarf that follows. Both scarves blend different colors, however, this scarf uses two yarns of the same texture. The next project uses two different colors and two different textures—one is a boucle yarn, the other is a thinner mohair yarn.

If you want to substitute your own choice of yarn, be sure to pay attention to texture as well as color. It goes without saying that both yarns must knit to approximately the same gauge. (In the following scarf, I used two strands of mohair yarn and one of the boucle to get the gauge.) If you do not pay attention to gauge, you will end up with a scarf that's thick and thin.

The two-color variation on brioche stitch can be a bit tricky but, like anything, it benefits from a step-by-step analysis.

First, an overview. To work two colors in this stitch, you must be able to begin a row at either end of the piece. That means a circular needle is required even though you'll be doing back and forth knitting.

The pattern can be divided into two segments, one for the wrong side and another for the right side of the work. Within each segment the yarn makes two passes, once with the main color, and again with the contrasting color. In each pass, work every other stitch, slipping the intervening stitches and at the same time carrying the working yarn along as a yarn-over.

INSTRUCTIONS

With MC, loosely cast on 11 sts.

Set-up row: (WS): sl1 purlwise for selvage, pick up CC, *k1, bring yarn to front, sl 1 st purlwise, yo needle to the back, repeat from * to last two sts. K 2.
Slide work to the opposite side of the circular needle and put it in your left hand

Row 1 (WS): With MC, Sl1, bring yarn to front,*sl 1, *yarn over needle to back and then bring yarn in front again, p next stitch along with the yo that straddles it, * until 1 st remains. P1. Turn work.

Row 2: (RS): With CC, sl1, *p next stitch along with yo straddling it, sl1p, yarn over needle to back and then bring yarn in front again, repeat from * until 2 sts remain. P next stitch along with yo straddling it, p1. Slide work to the other end of the needle and put needle in left hand.

Row 3: (RS): With MC, sl1, *bring yarn to front. Sl 1, yarn over needle to back, k next stitch along with yarn-over straddling it, repeat from* until 2 sts remain. Bring yarn to front, sl 1, yarn over needle to back, k1.
Turn work.

Row 4: (WS) With CC, sl1, *k1 along with yo straddling it, bring yarn to front, sl1p, yarn over needle to back, repeat from * until 1 st remains. Knit 1. Slide work to the other end of the needle. Repeat rows 1 to 4 for pattern.
Work until desired length.

Add fringe. Cut yarn twice the length desired for fringe, plus a little extra for knotting. Fold fringe in half. Inset a crochet hook from front to back of knitting and pull the folded fringe through to the front of the work, creating a loop. Then draw cut ends of fringe at back of work through the loop in front.

Left
A detailed view of the variegated yarn showing the texture and color variances.

Left
Using two colors in a brioche stitch pattern adds wonderful depth and dimension to your knitting. This shows combinations of knit, purl, and slipped stitches in a regimented ribbed pattern.

BEAUTIFUL BOUCLE

The contrasting color in this soft scarf is knitted in brioche stitch, with two strands together, creating a fabulous textural effect.

INSTRUCTIONS

With MC, loosely cast on 11 sts.

Set-up row: (WS): Sl1 purlwise for selvage, pick up CC, *k1, bring yarn to front, sl1 purlwise, yo needle to the back, repeat from * to last two sts. K 2.
Slide work to the opposite side of the circular needle and put it in your left hand.

Row 1 (WS): With MC, sl1, bring yarn to front,*sl1, *yarn over needle to back and then bring yarn in front again, p next stitch along with the yo that straddles it, * until 1 st remains. P 1. Turn work.

Row 2: (RS): With CC, sl1, *p next stitch along with yo straddling it, sl1p, yarn over needle to back and then bring yarn in front again, repeat from * until 2 sts remain. P next stitch along with yo straddling it, p 1. Slide work to the other end of the needle and put needle in left hand.

Row 3: (RS): With MC, sl1, *bring yarn to front. Sl1, yarn over needle to back, k next stitch along with yarn-over straddling it, repeat from* until 2 sts remain. Bring yarn to front, sl1, yarn over needle to back, k 1.
Turn work.

Row 4: (WS): With CC, sl1, *k 1 along with yo straddling it, bring yarn to front, sl1p, yarn over needle to back, repeat from * until 1 st remains. Knit 1. Slide work to the other end of the needle. Repeat rows 1 to 4 for pattern.

Skill level:	◼◼◼▢
Materials:	
Yarn:	Main Color: JCA Artful Yarns Circus, 93yd (85m)/3.5oz (100g) ball
	Contrasting Color: Classic Elite La Gran Mohair, 90yd (82m)/1.5oz(42g) ball
Color:	For MC: color 12
	For CC: color 6592
Amount:	1 ball MC, 2 balls CC (CC is used two strands together)
Total Yardage:	93yd (85m) for MC, 180yd (164.5m) for CC, including fringe
Needles:	US 15 (10mm)
Gauge:	Not necessary
Finished size:	Approx 4½" (11.5cm) wide and 78" (198cm) long, excluding fringe

Work until desired length. Add fringe. Cut yarn twice the length desired for fringe, plus a little extra for knotting. Fold fringe in half. Inset a crochet hook from front to back of knitting and pull folded fringe through to the front of the work, creating a loop. Then draw cut ends of fringe at back of work through the loop in front.

A SHIBORI SCARF

Shibori is a three-dimensional felting technique that gets its name from the Japanese approach to resist dyeing, in which a fabric is wrapped or folded and tied securely before it goes into the dye bath, often creating elaborate and intricate patterns. The art of tie-dyeing that was popular in the Sixties is a form of shibori.

Above
A detailed view of the various shapes created by the pebbles that were wrapped in knitted fabric. The background is felted, creating a marvellous textural contrast.

Skill level:	◼☐☐☐
Materials:	
Yarn:	Frog Tree Alpaca sport weight 130yd (119m)/1.75oz (50g)
Color:	98 Turquoise
Amount:	4 balls
Total Yardage:	520yd (476m)
Needles:	US 6 (4mm) or size to get gauge
Gauge:	20 sts and 28 rows = 4" (10cm) before felting
Other materials:	Assorted glass pebbles used in flower arrangements, or marbles, coins, milk-bottle lids or other small spheres Rubber bands
Finished size:	Approx: 5½" (14 cm) wide and 48" (122 cm) long, after felting

In felting, part of the knitted fabric, in its original state, is folded and tied securely, or wrapped tautly, around a small object. The immobilized portion of the fabric resists felting, leaving a pattern consisting of the sharp lines of the original knitting against a halo of softness.

INSTRUCTIONS

Cast on 44 sts, using backward loop method. Work in st st for approx. 80" (203cm). Bind off.

Prepare for felting and follow the instructions on the following page.

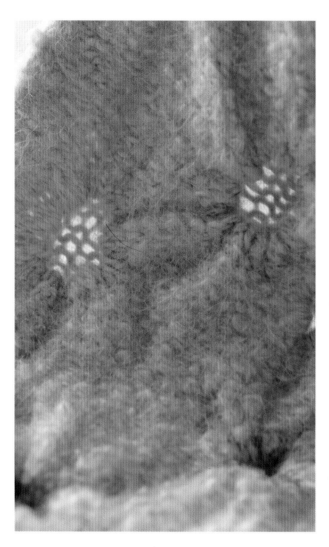

Above
Here you can see the back of the felted scarf, looking through the spaces left when the pebbles were removed.

With waste yarn, mark scarf off in thirds. On the outer two thirds of the scarf, place large and small oval glass pebbles or other spheres against the purl side of the fabric in the pattern of your choice and wrap the scarf around them, securing each one with a rubber band.

Felt according to instructions on page 32. Set the water level in the washing machine for a small load (glass pebbles do not break in a machine that's about one-third full of water) During felting, check the machine frequently and pull the fabric into a rectangular shape.

When the felting process is complete, remove the rubber bands and the pebbles. Block the finished scarf.

T I P

It is a good idea to work out the placement of the pebbles on paper before inserting them in the knitting to be felted. Mix large and small pebbles in proportion to each other, and make sure you balance the design at each end of the scarf. By that, I mean try to end up with approximately the same number of objects at each end.

Left
This photograph reveals the detail of the stockinette stitches that were wrapped around small pebbles during the felting process. A variety of pebble sizes adds visual appeal.

MEDALLION MOTIF FOR A MAN'S SCARF

Rich, embossed medallions cut a swath in this neckwarmer for your favorite guy—or for yourself. Traveling stitches and bobbles, framed in a simple garter stitch border, make for some interesting knitting.

Above
The raised cable pattern is shown here in detail. Note the softness of the yarn.

Skill level: ◖■■■◻

Materials

Yarn:	Classic Elite Inca Alpaca 109yd (100m)/1.75oz (50g)
Color:	1129 Blue
Amount:	5 skeins
Total yardage:	545yd (500m)
Needles:	US 7 (4.5mm) or size to get gauge
Gauge:	20 sts and 26 rows = 4" (10cm) in pattern stitch
Finished size:	Approx 8½" (21.5mm) wide and 55" (14cm) long

Special abbreviations:

M1P (M1 purl st): Pick up the horizontal bar between existing stitches and purl into back of it.

M1K (M1 knit stitch): Pick up the horizontal bar between existing stitches and knit into back of it.

B (Bobble—see chart): (K1, p1) twice into next st. Turn work. P4. Turn work. K4. Turn work. P4. Turn work. Sl2, k2 tog, p2sso.

C2B (Knit): Slip next st onto cable needle and hold at back of work. K next st from left-hand needle, then knit st off cn.

C2B (Purl): Slip next st onto cn and hold at back of work. P next st from left-hand needle, then k st off cn.

C2F (Knit): Slip next st onto cn and hold at front of work. K next st from left-hand needle, then knit st from cn.

C2F (Purl): Slip next st onto cn and hold at front of work. P next st from left-hand needle, then k st from cn.

C4B (Purl): Put next two sts on cn and hold to back. K2, p2 from cn.

C4F (Purl): Put next two sts on cn and hold to the front. P2. K2 from cn.

Above
The edge of the scarf has a ribbed pattern.

INSTRUCTIONS

Cast on 54 sts.

Edging:
Row 1: (RS): Knit.
Row 2: (See chart 1, starting from row 2): K3, p1, k 4, p2, k3, p1, k8, p1, k2, p4, k2, p1, k8, p1, k3, p2, k4, p1, k3.
Row 3: K4, p4, k2, p3, k1, p8, k1, p2, k4, p2, k1, p8, k1, p3, k2, p4, k4.
Rows 4, 6, and 8: Repeat row 2.
Rows 5 and 7: Repeat row 3.
Row 9: K3, M1k, k1, p4, k2, p3, M1p, k1, p8, k1, M1k, p2, k4, p2, k1, M1k, p8, k1, p1, M1p, p2, k2, p4, k1, M1k, k3. (60 sts)
Next Row: WS: K4, k the k sts and p the p sts of the previous row until 4 sts remain. K 4.

Work Rows 1 to 24 of medallion pattern (chart 2) until scarf is approx 55" (14cm) long, ending with row 24.
Next Row: (RS): Work Row 9 of edging chart. In place of marked increases, k2tog or p2tog, depending on the pattern stitch. Work 8 more rows of edging. Bind off.

KEY

B	Make bobble
☐	k on RS; P on WS
⊺	k every row (garter st)
⊡	p on RS; k on WS; K on WS
◤◥	C2F (purl)
◥◤	C2B (purl)
◤◥◤	C4B (purl)
◥◤◥	C4F (purl)
⧄⧄	C2B (knit)
⧅⧅	C2F (knit)
⊠	Make 1 knit stitch
⊠	Make 1 purl stitch

Chart 1, Man's medallion pattern

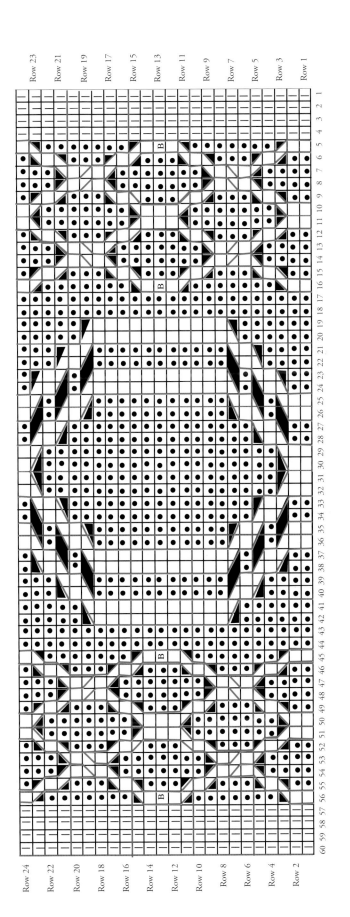

Chart 2, Man's medallion pattern

A CREAMY CABLE SCARF

A dark chocolate brown velvet ribbon running end to end up the center of a sea of oatmeal yarn adds elegance to the rich texture of this cabled scarf. The border along all edges adds the finishing touch.

Skill level:	■■■□
Materials:	
Yarn:	Classic Elite Princess 150yd (137m)/1.75 oz (50g) ball
Color:	3475 Beyond Beige
Amount:	4 balls
Total yardage:	600yd (548m)
Needles:	US 9 (5.5mm) or size to get gauge
Gauge:	26 sts and 25 rows = 4" (10cm) working k1, p1 rib
Finished size:	Length: 54"(137.5cm) Width: 8.5" (21.25cm)
Ribbon:	Chocolate brown velour ribbon 54½" (138cm)

Above
The central cable pattern has a stretch brown velvet ribbon run through it from end to end, adding a color contrast. You can choose any color you like.

SPECIAL ABBREVIATIONS

C4B: Put two sts on cable nedle (cn) and hold in back. K2 sts from left needle. K2 sts from cn.

C4F: Put 2 sts on cn and hold in front. K2 sts from left needle. K2 sts from cn.

C6B: Put 3 sts on cn and hold in back. K3 sts from left needle. K3 sts from cn.

C6F: Put 3 sts on cn and hold in front. K3 sts from left needle. K3 sts from cn.

INSTRUCTIONS

Cast on 65 sts (including 2 selvage sts). Work k1 selvage st at each end of every row throughout. Note: These sts are not included in the following pattern but are included in the stitch count.

Work in k1, p1 ribbing for 7 rows.

Increase row: (WS): P1, k1 rib for 6 sts, M1, k1, p8, M1, k2, p4, k2, p1,M1, p7, k1, p9, k1, M1, p4, k2, p3, M1, p5, k1,M1, k1, p1, k1, p1, k1, p1. (6 sts increased). Total 71 sts

Next sequence:
Row 1: K1,p1 rib for 6 sts, p2, k3, C6F, p2, C4B, p2, k3, C6B, yo, put next 4 sts on cable needle and hold to front, k3, k2 tog from cable needle, k remaining 2 sts from cable needle, k3, p2, C4F, p2, k3, C6F, p2, *p1, k1 repeat from * to end.

Row 2: Knit the knit stitches and purl the purl sts. Knit into yarn-over at center.

Row 3: K1, p1 rib for 6 sts, p2, C6B, k3, p2, C4B, p2, C6B, k3, p1, k3, C6F, p2, C4F, p2, C6B, k3, p2, *p1, k1 repeat from * to end.

Row 4: Knit the knit stitches and purl the purl stitches.

Row 5: K1, p1, rib for 6 sts, p2, k3, C6F, p2, C4B, p2, k9, p1, k9, p2, C4F, p2, k3, C6F, p2, *p1, k1 repeat from * to end.

Row 6: Repeat Row 4.

Row 7: K1, p1, rib for 6 sts, p2, C6B, k3, p2, C4B, p2, k9, p1, k9, p2, C4F, p2, C6B, k3, p2, *p1, k1 repeat from * to end.

Row 8: Repeat Row 4.

Repeat rows 1 to 8 for pattern 40 times or until scarf measures 52½" from cast-on edge, ending on a Row 7.

Decrease row: (WS): P1, k1 rib for 6 sts, k2tog, p7, p2tog, k2, p4, k2, p1, p2tog, p6, k1, p6, p2tog, p1, k2, p2, p2tog, k2, p3, p2tog, p4, k2 * k1, p1 repeat from * to end of row. (65sts)
Work in k1, p1 ribbing for 7 rows.
Bind off.

Finishing:
Starting at the end of the ribbing and leaving 1" (2.5cm) of ribbon at the back of the scarf, thread the ribbon through the yarn over loops along the center of the scarf. Push the other end of the ribbon through the hole where the cable ends and the ribbing begins again. Secure the ribbon at each end with a few neatly sewn stitches.

Opposite page
A combination of cable crossings
adds rich texture to this scarf.

A LUSCIOUS LACY SCARF

This lacy scarf whispers luxury and sophistication with its undulating borders and tapered edges. The scarf is worked in a wavy leaf pattern in two sections, from the center outward, by picking up stitches for the second section from the first section's cast on edge.

Skill level: ■■■◻

Materials

Yarn:	Rowan Kidsilk Night 227yd (208m)/87oz (50g)
Color:	610 Starry night
Amount:	2 balls
Total yardage:	454yd (416m)
Needles:	Size US 3 (3.25mm)
Finished size:	8" (20cm) wide 52" (132cm) long
Other:	Waste yarn

Notes: The undulating edges of the scarf raise a couple of issues. These wavy edges are achieved by using three and a half repeats of the stitch pattern across the width of the scarf. This is important information for placing markers to divide the beginning and end of the stitch pattern.

On chart 1, a green line marks the appropriate spots for these markers. They may seem off-center, but they're really not. Notice, because of the shifting pattern, that the markers also shift one stitch to the left on Row 13, and then shift back again on Row 15.

INSTRUCTIONS

Begin at center of the scarf. Using waste yarn and a provisional cast on (*see pages 16 and 17*) cast on 45 sts.

Foundation row: K2, p until 2 sts remain. K2. Turn.

Work Row 1 of chart 1, including right border, three and a half pattern repeats, and left border. Place markers between pattern repeats.

Row 2 and all alternate rows throughout the entire pattern (not charted): K 2, purl until 2 stitches remain, k2.

Work all elements of chart 1, as established, 10 times, or until piece is slightly less than half desired length.

Work chart 2 through Row 35. 3 sts remain. Sl2, k2 tog, p2sso. Break off yarn and weave tail into the border.

Return to the center and slowly unravel the provisional cast on, picking up stitches of the project yarn as you go. (42 sts)
K2, p8, M1, p11, M1, p11, M1, p8, k2.

Beginning with Row 1, work chart 1 the same as for the first section of the scarf. Work chart 2 as in the first section.

Block the scarf gently. Lay the piece flat, folded in half if necessary. Weigh down wavy edges with coins or other small weights. Spray with water. Allow to dry.

Chart 2: Scarf End

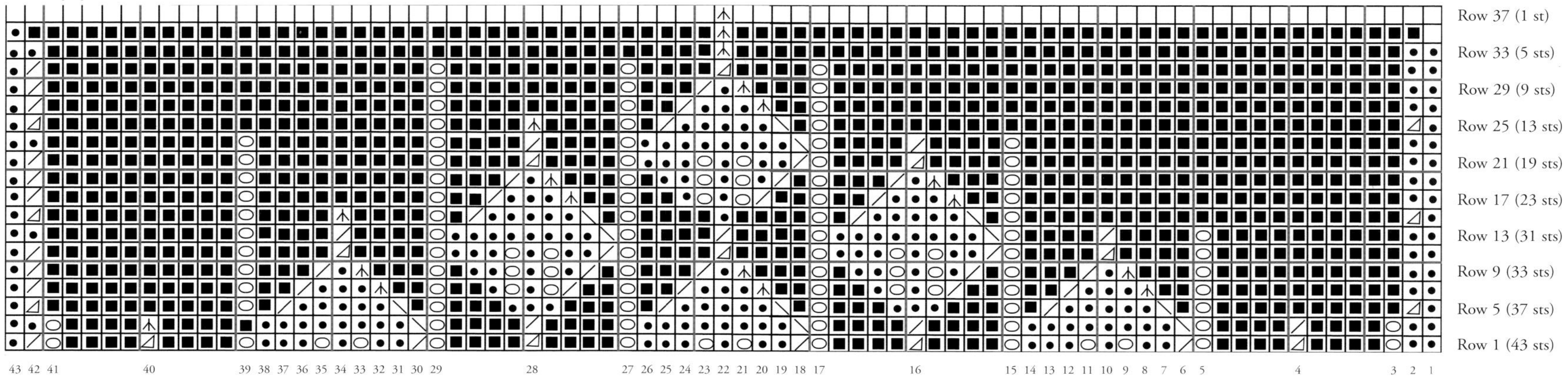

Row 37 (1 st)
Row 33 (5 sts)
Row 29 (9 sts)
Row 25 (13 sts)
Row 21 (19 sts)
Row 17 (23 sts)
Row 13 (31 sts)
Row 9 (33 sts)
Row 5 (37 sts)
Row 1 (43 sts)

3 2 1
4
6 5
8 7
10 9
12 11
15 14 13
16
18 17
20 19
22 21
24 23
26 25
28
27
30 29
32 31
34 33
36 35
38 37
40
39
43 42 41

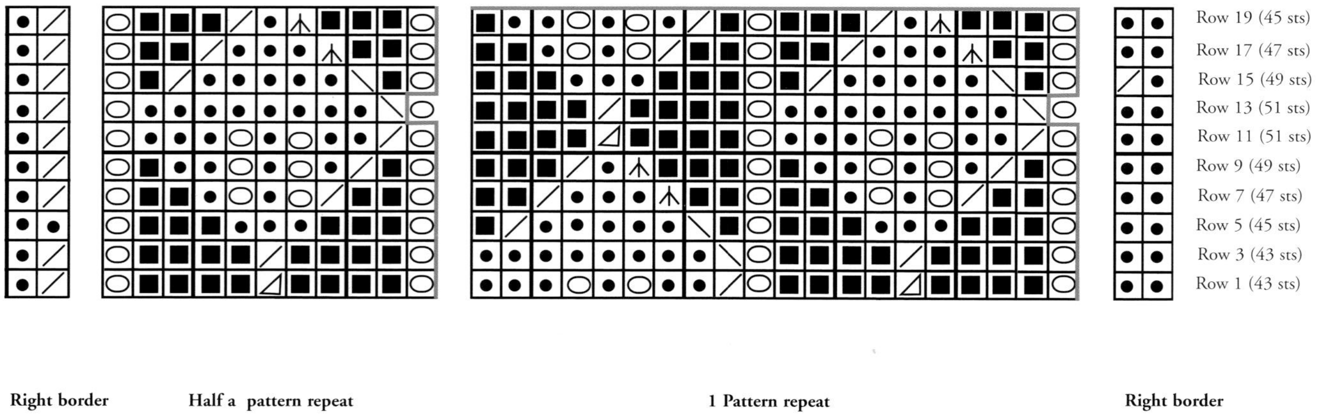

KEY

- ☐• Knit
- ■ No stitch
- ◹ Knit 2 together
- ◸ SSK slip 2 stitches together then knit together
- ⊀ Slip 2 sts as if to k2tog, knit next, pass the slipped sts over as one
- ◯ Yarn over
- ◺ Slip 2 sts as if to k2tog, knit next 2 sts tog, pass the slipped sts over as one

Chart 1: Open work Pattern

Row 19 (45 sts)
Row 17 (47 sts)
Row 15 (49 sts)
Row 13 (51 sts)
Row 11 (51 sts)
Row 9 (49 sts)
Row 7 (47 sts)
Row 5 (45 sts)
Row 3 (43 sts)
Row 1 (43 sts)

Right border

1 Pattern repeat

Half a pattern repeat

Right border

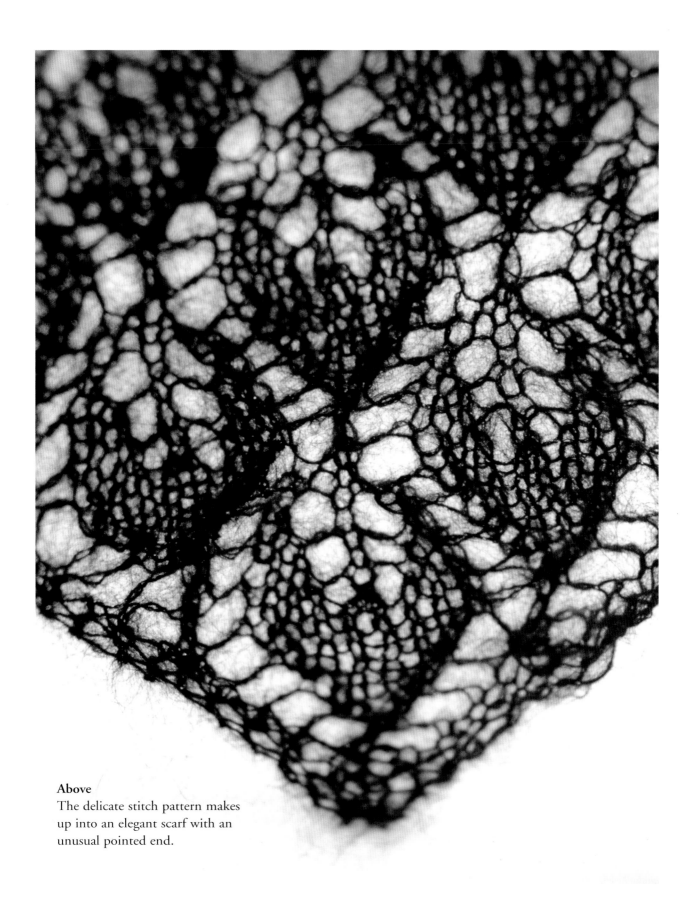

Above
The delicate stitch pattern makes
up into an elegant scarf with an
unusual pointed end.

ACCESSORIES

In this chapter you will find a collection of interesting

accessories including an evening bag knitted in silk ribbon,

and two designs for a four-legged friend.

MODERN MUFFATEES

These vintage-style arm warmers are incredibly soft, warm, and just a bit naughty! They are knit in the round, beginning with a lacy ruffle at the wrist, using two strands of a lace-weight yarn to add substance and warmth.

Above
The soft yarn combined with the open weave stitch pattern makes an attractive ruffle at the wrist.

Skill level: ■■■□
Materials
Yarn: Filatura di Crosa Baby Kid Extra 268yd (245m)/.87oz (25g)
Color: 474 Black
Amount: 2 balls, used two strands held together
Total yardage: 536yd (490m)
Needles: One set double-pointed needles US 5 (3.75mm) or size to get gauge
US size 6 (4mm) for casting on and binding off, or one size larger than used for knitting
Gauge: 30 rows and 22 sts = 4" (10cm)
Finished size: 9" (23cm) in circumference at widest part of forearm.
9" (23cm) long from wrist to elbow.

Stitch Patterns
For Ruffle at Wrist: (16 sts)

Round 1: *K2, yo twice, [sl1, k1, psso], k2tog, yo twice, double vertical decrease (sl2, k1, p2sso) k3 tog, yo twice, [sl1, k1, psso], k2tog, yo twice, repeat from * to end.

Round 2: *K2, p1, k1 into double yarn-over, repeat from * to end.

Repeat these two rounds for ruffle pattern.

Lace Pattern for arm: (12 sts)
Round 1: *K1, yo, sl1k, k1, psso, k3, yo, sl1k, k1,psso, k2, k2 tog, yo, repeat from * to end.

Rounds 2, 4, and 6: Knit.

Round 3: *K1, yo, [sl1, k1, psso], k1, k2tog, yo, k1, yo, [sl1, k1, psso], k1, k2tog, yo, repeat from * to end.

Round 5: *K1, yo, [sl1, k1, psso], k2 tog, yo, k3, yo, [sl1, k1, psso], k2tog, yo, repeat from * to end.

Ruffle
Using larger needles, cast on 96 sts. Divide sts among three or four smaller double-pointed needles.

Work in ruffle pattern until piece measures 3" (6.5cm).

Next round: *K3 tog, k3 tog, k2 tog, repeat from * (36sts.)

Change to lace pattern for arm.
Work 10 rounds even.

Round 11: Increase 1 k st at the beginning and the end.

Continue in lace pattern, increasing one knit stitch at beginning and end of every 10th round 5 times more (48 sts). Work even in lace pattern (4 repeats) until piece measures 8½" (21.5cm) from wrist or ½" (1.25cm) short of desired length. K 1 round, p 1 round, k 1 round, p 1 round. Bind off loosely with larger needles.

Lace Pattern For Arm Chart

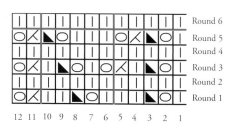

KEY

◿ K3 tog

— purl

| knit

⅄ Sl2tog knitwise, k1, p2sso

○ yarn over

⟋ k2tog

◣ sl1, k1, psso (SKP)

Lace Pattern For Ruffle Chart

Left
The muffattee can
reach up to the elbow,
depending on the
length of the forearm.

WOW-FACTOR DOG SWEATER

A lucky small dog will look elegant in this Aran-style sweater as it steps out for a constitutional. The main body is done in a raised trinity stitch which gives the sweater an interesting texture. A cabled rib in an off-white around the neck and body area finishes off the piece.

Skill level: ◼◼◼▭
Materials
Yarn: Cascade 220 Superwash 220yd (201m)/100g(3.5oz)
Color: For color A: 815 Black
For color B: 817 Ivory
Amount: 1 ball of each
Total Yardage: 220yd (201m) for A, 220yd (201m) for B
Needles: US 8 (5mm)straight needles, or size to obtain gauge
US 6 (4mm) double pointed needles
US 6 (4mm) circular needle 16" (40.6cm) long
Stitch Markers: 2
Gauge: 18 sts and 25 rows = 4" (10cm) in trinity st on size 8 needles
26 sts and 26 rows = 4" (10cm) in cable rib on size 6 needles
Finished Size: Chest circumference = 13" (15¼", 17½") [33cm (39cm, 44.5cm)] Length from nape of neck to tail: 11" (12", 13") [28cm (30.5cm, 33cm)]

Note: See Page 94 for instructions on how to measure your dog.

Pattern stitches
Trinity stitch: Multiple of four
Row 1 and 3: Purl
Row 2: (WS) *(K1,p1,k1) into first stitch, p 3 tog, repeat from * to end.
Row 4: *P3 tog, (k1,p1, k1) into next st, repeat from * to end.

Cable rib: Multiple of 14
Set-up row (WS) *K2, p8, k2, p2, repeat from * to end
Row 1: (RS) *P 2, C4B, C4F, p2, k2, repeat from * to end.
Rows 2 and 4: Knit the knit stitches and purl the purl stitches.
Row 3: P2, C4F, C4B, p2, k2, repeat from * to end.

INSTRUCTIONS

Using size 6 needles and color B, cast on 64 (78, 86) sts. Maintaining a selvage stitch at each end, work 56 (70, 84) sts in cable rib pattern, reserving 4 (4, 0) additional sts at each end for k2, p2 rib.

Work in pattern, as established, for 4 pattern repeats, ending with ws row.

Next row: Drop B and pick up A. Work first row of Trinity stitch, increasing 14, (16, 28) sts, evenly spaced across row. 78 (94, 114) sts

Work in Trinity stitch for 1" (1½", 1½") [2.5cm (3.8cm, 2.8cm)] ending on WS row.

Divide for legs.
Side section:
Next row:
For all three sizes: Work 1 selvage st, work next 12 sts in pattern, work another selvage st, and put remaining sts on holder. Turn work.
Maintaining 1 selvage st at each end, work in trinity stitch on intervening 12 sts for 2" (2½", 2½") ending with WS row. Break yarn.

Center section:
For all three sizes, bind off next 14 sts. Work 1 selvage st. Work next 20 (36, 56) sts in pattern. Work another selvage stitch. Turn work.
Maintaining selvage stitches, work in trinity st on these 22 (38, 58) sts for 2" (2½", 2½") ending with WS row. Break yarn.

Side section:
For all three sizes, bind off 14 sts. Work 1 selvage st. Work next 12 sts in pattern. Work another selvage st. Turn work.
Work in trinity st on these 14 sts for 2" (2½", 2½") [5cm (6.5cm, 6.5cm)] ending with WS row.

Rejoin sections:
Work 1 selvage sts. Purl across 13 sts, cast on 14 sts to cover gap, purl center 22 (38, 58) sts, cast on 14 sts to cover gap, purl across 13 sts, work 1 selvage st.

Continue working in trinity st pattern until piece measures 5" (6", 6") [12.5cm (15.25cm, 15.25cm)] from base of ribbing, or 1½" (4cm) shorter than desired length. End with WS row.

Above
A cable rib edging in white creates a contrast with the black trinity stitch used for the body. The edging goes around the neck and the entire body shape.

Shape tail section:
For all three sizes: Bind off 10 sts at beginning of next 2 rows. 58 (74, 94) sts

Next row: (RS): Work 1 selvage st, P3 tog, work until 4 sts remain. P3 tog, work selvage st. Maintaining selvage sts, work double decrease each side on every other row 3 (5, 7) times more. 42 (50, 62) sts

Work even until piece measures 9½" (10½", 11½") [24cm (26.5cm, 29cm)] or about 1½" (4cm) shorter than desired length, ending with WS row.

Next row: Ssk twice, bind off 8 (9, 14) sts, work to end. 32 (39, 48) sts
Next row: Ssk twice, bind off 8 (9, 14) sts work to end. 22 (28, 34) sts
Bind off remaining 22 (28, 34) sts.

Finish leg openings: Pick up 34 (42, 42) sts around each leg opening. For smaller size, work 2 repeats of cable rib and the remaining sts in k2, p2 rib. For larger sizes, work 3 pattern repeats of cable rib. Work until cuffs are about 1" (2.5cm) long. Bind off.

Sew center front seam.

Finishing for tail section:
Prepare to work in cable rib. First, using waste yarn, mark the two rear outside corners where bound-off stitches begin.

Use color B and size 6 circular needle. Starting at the center seam, pick up 28 (36, 40) sts to the first piece of waste yarn, place marker. Pick up 42 (54, 60) sts between marker and 2nd piece of waste yarn, place marker. Pick up 28 (36, 40)sts between marker and seam.

Set up round: *p2, k8, p2, k2; rep from * to end. Note: For smallest size only, k2, work set up round to last 2 sts, k2.
For smallest size only, maintain 2 knit sts at each end of every round.
For all sizes, make sure the markers are placed in between 2 knit sts. Move markers along slightly if necessary.

Work even cable rib for 2 rounds.

Round 3: *Work to 1 st before marker, inc 1, work 2 sts, inc 1; rep from *. Work to end of round.
Round 4: Work even.
Round 5: Repeat round 3.
Round 6: Work even.
Round 7: Repeat round 3.
Round 8: Bind off.

Above
A detail of the cuff at the leg openings. These can be made shorter or longer depending upon the length of the dog's leg.

T I P

To make sure that the main body of the garment and the ribbing lie flat, follow these two rules for picking up stitches:

When working across the top or bottom of the knitting, pick up one stitch for each stitch above or below.

When working along the side, pick up 3 sts for every 4 rows.

Wow-Factor Dog Sweater

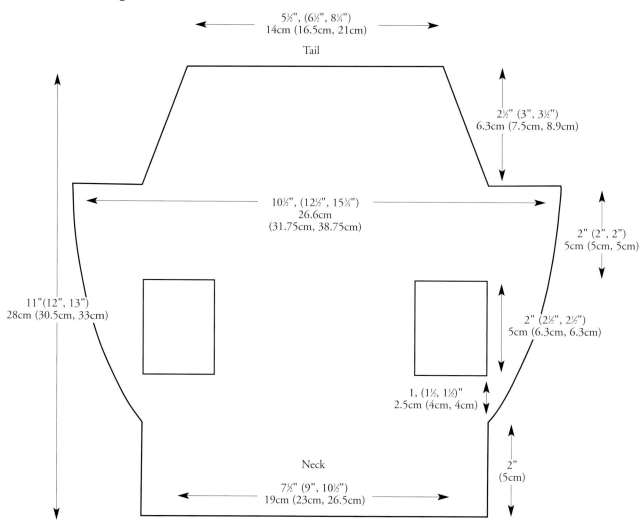

5½", (6½", 8¼")
14cm (16.5cm, 21cm)

Tail

2½" (3", 3½")
6.3cm (7.5cm, 8.9cm)

10½", (12½", 15¾")
26.6cm
(31.75cm, 38.75cm)

2" (2", 2")
5cm (5cm, 5cm)

11" (12", 13")
28cm (30.5cm, 33cm)

2" (2½", 2½")
5cm (6.3cm, 6.3cm)

1, (1½, 1½)"
2.5cm (4cm, 4cm)

Neck

2"
(5cm)

7½" (9", 10½")
19cm (23cm, 26.5cm)

MEASURING YOUR DOG

Dogs, it is obvious, do not come in standard sizes. The measurements presented here for our two woof-warmers are only guidelines.

To ensure a proper fit, be sure to measure your dog before beginning one of the sweaters on these pages. Here are a number of measurements necessary to guarantee a good fit.

The three most critical measurements are:
1. The neck circumference, plus 1" (2.5cm) to this measurement for ease

2. The length of the back, from the nape of the neck to the base of the tail
3. The circumference of the chest at its fullest part, plus 1" (2.5cm) to this measurement for ease

Also helpful are the following measurements:.
1. The distance from the base of the neck to the top of the fore legs
2. The distance between the fore legs
3. The distance from the base of the neck down the front of the chest to the sternum, the point where the ribcage ends

GLAMOROUS LEGWARMERS

A chevron stitch is used to create a striking border that can be worn either at the bottom or the top. A slip-stitch rib creates a wonderful vertical line along the calf.

Pattern note: This chevron pattern has been modified to enable you to work in the round and eliminate a seam. The pattern has two rounds; one for decreases and another for increases, which, when combined, give the chevron its distinctive zigzag. In the increases round, the first stitch of each pattern repeat is slipped, and in the decreases round, it is worked. But, the first stitch of each round is worked twice in the round earmarked for decreases, once at the beginning and a second time at the end. It is not worked at all in the succeeding round.

INSTRUCTIONS

Begin at top:
With color A, cast on 72 (84, 96)sts.
Round 1: Ssk, *knit 9, sl2, k1, p2sso, repeat from* until 1 st remains. K2tog, inserting needle knitwise through the first stitch of round.
Round 2: Beginning with second stitch in round, *p4, in next st (p1, yo, p1,) p4, sl1p wyib, repeat from * ending with p 4.
Round 3: Repeat round 1.
Round 4: Repeat round 2.
Round 5: Repeat round 1.
Round 6: Beginning with second stitch in round, *k4, in next st (k1, yo, k1,), k4, sl1p wyib, repeat from * ending with k4.
Round 7: Drop A, pick up color B. Repeat. round 1.
Round 8: Repeat round 2.
Round 9. Drop B. Pick up color C. Repeat round 1.
Round 10. Repeat round 6.
Round 11: Drop C. Pick up color D. Repeat round 1.

Skill level:	◼◼◼◻

Materials:

Yarn:	Jo Sharp Classic DK Wool 107yd (98m)/1.75oz(50g)
Color:	Color A, 503 Amethyst
	Color B, 301 Natural
	Color C, 349 Porcelain
	Color D, 346 Seashell
Amount:	For A, 6 (8, 9) balls
	For B, C, and D, 1 ball each
Total Yardage:	642yd (856yd, 963yd) 588 (784m, 882m)] for A; 107yd (98m) for each of B, C, and D
Needles:	US 6 (4mm)or size to obtain gauge
Gauge:	26.5 sts and 28 rows = 4" chevron pattern
Finished Size:	Circumference is 11", (12¾", 14½") [28, (32.5cm, 37cm). Length is 13" (33cm)

Round 12: Repeat round 2.
Round 13: Drop D. Pick up C. Repeat round 1.
Round 14: Repeat round 6.
Round 15: Drop C. Pick up B. Repeat round 1.
Round 16: Repeat round 2
Round 17: Drop B. Pick up A. Repeat round 1.
Round 18 and all even-numbered rounds: repeat round 6.
Round 19 and odd-numbered rounds: repeat round 1.

Work even using A until piece measures 13" (33cm) or desired length. Bind off.

A FAIR ISLE DOG SWEATER

This soft and thick Fair Isle sweater—long enough to cover the hindquarters—will please any fashion-conscious dog and its owner!

INSTRUCTIONS

Note: This pattern requires you to read the charts (see page 101) and allow for shaping and leg openings at the same time according to the size you are knitting. You might find it easier to mark off the rows as you knit.

Neck:
With smaller straight needles and color B, cast on 48 (54, 64) sts. This includes 2 selvage sts.
Work k2, p2 rib for 1½".
On last row inc 22 (26, 26) sts evenly spaced (70, 80, 90 sts)

Drop B and pick up A. Switch to larger needles. Work in st st, incorporating fair isle pattern while shaping sweater.

The sequence for the fair isle pattern is as follows:
7 rows in plain stockinette, using A.
7 rows collar pattern (chart 1).
7 rows in plain stockinette, using A.
10 rows dog chart (chart 2)
7 rows in plain stockinette, using A.
7 rows collar pattern (chart 1).
Remainder of sweater is in plain stockinette, using A.

At the same time, shape sweater as follows:
Work in St st until piece measures 3" (3", 3½") [7.5cm (7.5cm, 9cm)] in length, ending with a WS row.

Begin shaping holes for front legs:
Next row: K 8 (9, 9) sts. Put remaining sts on holder. Work back and forth on 8 (9, 9) sts until

Skill level:	◖■■■▭
Materials	
Yarn:	Debbie Bliss Cashmerino Aran 100yd (91m)/1.75oz (50g)
Color:	For A, 101 Cream
	For B, 607 Purple
	For C, 601 Lilac
Amount:	For A, 2 balls
	For B, 2 balls
	For C, 1 ball
Total yardage:	200yd (182m) for A, 200yd (182m) for B, 100yd (91m) for C
Needles:	One pair straight needles US 8 (5mm) or size to get gauge
	One pair straight needles US 6 (4mm) or size to get gauge
	One set 4 or 5 double-pointed needles US 6 (4mm) or size to get gauge
	One 16" (40mm) long circular needle US 6 (4mm) or size to get gauge
Gauge:	19 sts and 22 rows = 4" (10cm) in fair isle pattern

this section is 2" (2½", 3") [5cm (6.5cm, 7.5cm] long, ending with WS row. Put sts on holder.

Attach new strand of yarn and bind off next 9 (9, 9) sts. Work center 36 (44, 54) sts until this section is 2" (2½", 3") [5cm (6.5cm, 7.5cm)] long, ending with WS row. Break yarn.

Re-attach yarn and bind off next 9 (9, 9) sts. Work side section of 8 (9, 9) sts until it is 2" (2½", 3") [5cm (6.5cm, 7.5cm)] long, ending with WS row.

Next row: Keeping in fair isle pattern, work side 8 (9, 9) sts, cast on 9 (9, 9) sts over gap formed by bind-off, work center 36 (44, 54) sts, cast on 9 (9, 9) sts over gap formed by bind-off, work last 8 (9, 9) sts.

Work even until piece measures 6" (6½", 7") [15.25cm (16.5cm, 17.75cm)] or desired length over belly, measured along selvedge.

Shape Tail:
Bind of 8 (8, 8) sts at the beginning of each of the next 2 rows. 54 (64, 74 sts).

Dec 1 st each side, every other row 8 (10, 12) times. 38 (44, 50 sts)

Work even until piece measures 9" (11", 13") [25.5cm (30.5cm, 35.5cm)] from beginning, or desired length, ending with a WS row.

Next row: Ssk, ssk, bind off 7 (8, 10) sts, work to end.
Next row: P2tog, p2tog, bind off 7 (8, 10) sts, purl to end.
Next row: Bind off center 24 (28, 30) sts.

Finish holes for front legs:
Using B and double-pointed needles, pick up 36 (40, 44) sts around each hole and work in k2, p2 rib for 1". Bind off.

Finish tail section:
Prepare to work in k2, p2 ribbing. First, using waste yarn, mark two rear outside corners where bound-off stitches begin.
Using purple yarn and circular needle, pick up 72 (100, 116) sts around belly and tail section. Pick up a few extra stitches at marked corners, if necessary, to ensure that two knit stitches are at each corner.

Work in k2, p2 ribbing for 2 rounds.

Round 3: Inc 1 st purl-wise before and after each of the two rear corners.

Round 4: Work even

Round 5: Repeat round 3

Round 6: Work even

Round 7: Repeat round 3

Round 8: Bind off.

Below
A detail of the dog pattern against the cream background. The bottom photograph shows the ribbing around the neck.

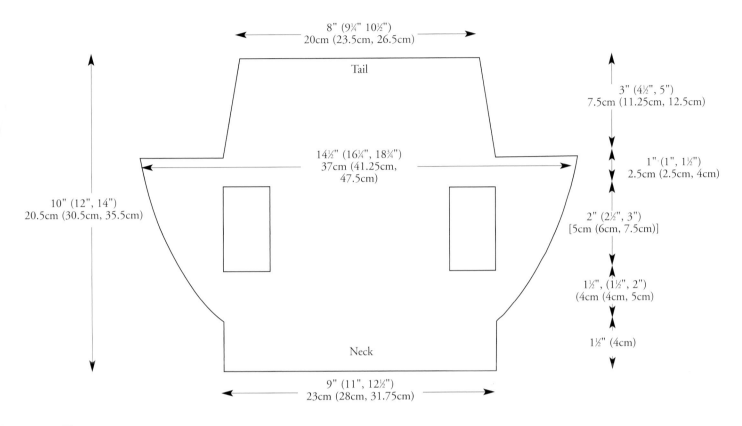

8" (9¼" 10½")
20cm (23.5cm, 26.5cm)

Tail

3" (4½", 5")
7.5cm (11.25cm, 12.5cm)

14½" (16¼", 18¾")
37cm (41.25cm, 47.5cm)

1" (1", 1½")
2.5cm (2.5cm, 4cm)

10" (12", 14")
20.5cm (30.5cm, 35.5cm)

2" (2½", 3")
[5cm (6cm, 7.5cm)]

1½", (1½", 2")
(4cm, 4cm, 5cm)

1½" (4cm)

Neck

9" (11", 12½")
23cm (28cm, 31.75cm)

Chart 1

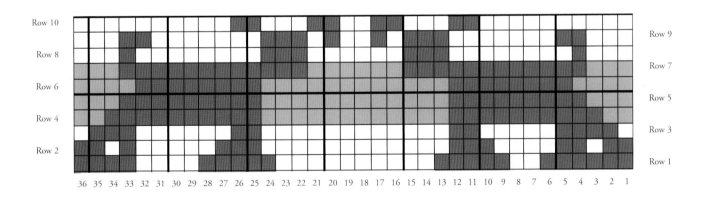

Row 10   Row 9

Row 8   Row 7

Row 6   Row 5

Row 4   Row 3

Row 2   Row 1

36 35 34 33 32 31 30 29 28 27 26 25 24 23 22 21 20 19 18 17 16 15 14 13 12 11 10 9 8 7 6 5 4 3 2 1

Chart 2

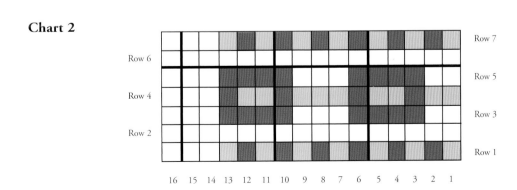

Row 7

Row 6   Row 5

Row 4   Row 3

Row 2   Row 1

16 15 14 13 12 11 10 9 8 7 6 5 4 3 2 1

A SOFT BAND OF ROSES

This cloud of a headband, made with a supersoft alpaca blend, is wide enough to cover your ears on a winter's walk. It is made on smaller-than-usual needles to minimize stretch and ensure a snug fit. The satin flowers make this très chic!

Skill level: ■□□□

Materials:

Yarn:	Plymouth Yarns Baby Alpaca Brush 110yd (100.5m) 1.75oz/50g
Color	1000
Amount:	2 balls
Total yardage:	220yd (198m)
Needles:	1 US 7 (4.5mm) circular needle 16" (40cm) long, or size to get gauge
	1 US 9 (5.5mm) circular needle 16" (40cm) long, or 2 sizes larger to get gauge
Finished size:	18½" (47cm) in circumference Fits most adult heads when stretched
Gauge:	15 sts and 28 rows = 4" (10cm) using size 7 needles
Trim:	Small satin roses

INSTRUCTIONS

Using larger needles, cast on 69 sts very loosely to allow for necessary stretch. Place marker to mark beginning of rounds.

Hem:
Knit 1 round with larger needles. Switch to smaller needles. Knit 3 more rounds

Picot edge:
Next round: *K1, yo, k2 tog, repeat from * to end.

Knit until piece measures 3" (7.5cm) from picot edge.

Next round: Make second picot edge, the same as the first.

Hem: K 3 rounds.
Switch to larger needles and knit one more round. Bind off very loosely.

Fold headband at picot edges and loosely sew hems to wrong side. Stitch small satin flowers or another preferred embellishment (such as sequins) along the edge to finish off the headband.

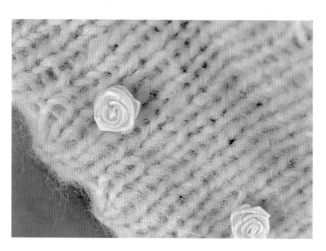

Left
Delicate small satin roses turn this practical and warm headband into a dressy affair.

ACCESSORIZE WITH COLOR

This dazzling evening clutch will be the only accessory you need on a special night on the town. The bag is worked in ribbon yarn in a plaited stitch that adds texture as well as body, and is worked in two pieces to accommodate the directional stitch.

Pattern Stitch: (Multiple of 3+1)

Row 1: K1, *Insert needle purlwise throughout the next stitch and knitwise into the second st on left needle. K the second st, but leave both loops on left needle. Knit 1st st on left needle through the back loop. Drop both sts from left needle. K1, repeat from* until 1 st remains. K1. Turn.

Row 2: P2, *p2 tog, and leave both sts on left needle; move right needle between the two sts just purled together and p first st again. Drop both sts from needle, p1 repeat from * to end.

INSTRUCTIONS

Make 2 pieces.
Cast on 43 sts.
Set-up row: Purl until 1 st remains. P in back and front of this st. With backward loop method (*see page 17*), cast on 1 st. (45 st) Turn.
Row 1: K in front and back of first st, (46 sts), k1. K1, *Insert needle purlwise throught the next stitch and knitwise into the second st on left needle. K the second st, but leave both loops on left needle. K the 1st st on left needle through the back loop. Drop both sts from left needle. K1, repeat from* until 1 st remains. K in front and back of last st. Using backward loop method, cast on 1 st (48 sts). Turn.

Row 2: P in front and back of first st (49 sts), *p2 tog and leave both sts on left needle; move right needle between the two sts just purled together

Skill level: ◼◼◼◻
Materials
Yarn: Berroco Yoga 119yd (110m)/1.75oz (50g)
Color: 6406 Maharishi
Yarn amount: 2 balls incl. yardage for swatch
Total yardage: 238yd (220m)
Needles: US 9 (5.5mm) or size to get gauge
Tapestry needle
Large sewing needle
Gauge: 22.5 sts and 28 rows = 4"
Purse frame: LS 60 in gold
9" (28cm) fabric for lining
Finished size: Approx. 9¼" (23cm) wide at bottom; 5½" (14cm) tall assembled. Unassembled, 9½" (24cm) wide, 5¾" (14.5cm) tall

and p first st again. Drop both sts from needle, p1 repeat from * to end. Return last st to left needle. P in front and back of this st. using backward loop method, cast on 1 st (51 sts). Turn.

Row 3: K in front and back of first st, (52 sts), k1. K1, *insert needle purlwise through the next stitch and knitwise into the second st on left needle. K the second st, but leave both loops on left needle. Knit 1st st on left needle through the back loop. Drop both sts from left needle. K1, repeat from* until 1 st remains. K in front and back of last st. Using backward loop method, cast on 1 st. (54 sts) Turn.

Row 4: P in front and back of first st (55 sts), *p2 tog, and leave both sts on left needle; move right needle between the two sts just purled together and purl first st again. Drop both sts from needle, p1 repeat from * to end.

Work even on 55 sts in pattern as established for 30 rows, ending with WS row.
Next Row: Bind off in pattern stitch as follows: K1, *insert right needle purlwise throughout the next stitch and knitwise into the second st on left needle. K the second st, but leave both loops on left needle. Knit 1st st on left needle through the back loop. Drop both sts from left needle. Return 1st st on right needle back onto left needle, pass second st on right needle over 1st st on right needle. Return 1st st on left needle to right needle. Pass second st on right needle over 1st st. K1, pass second on right needle over first st on right needle. Repeat from * until all sts have been bound off. Fasten off.

To assemble bag:
Lining
Use one bag piece to create a pattern for fabric lining. First, put the knitted piece on paper and draw a line around the circumference. This will be the sewing line. Add ¼" (0.6cm) all around the

sewing line for a seam allowance. Cut out pattern along the outer line and pin it to a double thickness of fabric. Cut out fabric on cutting line.

With right sides of lining together, sew along sides and bottom. Turn over ¼" (0.6cm) of fabric along top of bag, with raw edges on the wrong side. Press. Machine stitch close to folded edge. Set aside lining.

Assemble knitted pieces:
With scrap yarn, mark sewing lines along bottom and sides of knitted pieces. On the bottom of the bag, the sewing line should be between the first and second row. On the sides, the sewing line should be along the bars between the edge stitch and the second stitch.

Line up one knitted bag piece over the other, with right sides out. Using tapestry needle and ribbon yarn, sew pieces together from the right side, working along the bottom first then the sides from bottom to top using mattress stitch.

Attach lining to bag:
Fit the lining inside the bag, with wrong side of lining to wrong side of bag. With sewing thread and needle, stitch lining to bag about ¼" (0.6cm) below the top edge of the knitting.

Attach bag to purse frame:

Put the purse frame inside the bag. On one side, position the knitted fabric so that the middle lines up with the center of the purse frame. Using scrap yarn, temporarily attach the middle of the knitted fabric to one of the two center holes of the purse frame.

Thread a tapestry needle with ribbon yarn. Begin working in the lower right corner of the purse frame as it faces you. Draw the ribbon yarn from the inside out through the first hole and through the knitted fabric. Then insert the needle from the outside in through the fabric and the purse frame. Continue this in-and-out motion, drawing the yarn through tightly at every stitch, until you have reached the bottom left hole on the side facing you. Then reverse direction and work back to the starting point so that no metal shows between the holes in the purse frame on the inside of the bag. Knot the beginning and end of the yarn and hide the tails under the line of stitches on the inside of the purse frame.

In the same manner, sew the other side of the bag to the purse frame.

Bag Chart

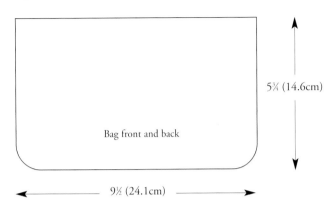

5¾ (14.6cm)

Bag front and back

9½ (24.1cm)

Left
I selected the color of the lining to repeat one of the colors in the ribbon yarn.

GLOVES

Fingers need to be warm in winter. On the following pages you will discover how to make the cutest mittens as well as fingered gloves. Good luck!

GORGEOUS GLOVES

These red women's gloves will add a little dash to a gray day. They're made from a soft but sturdy workhorse yarn and embellished with a decorative stitch, with pearls decorating the cuff.

INSTRUCTIONS

Cast on 40 sts and divide them evenly between 3 or 4 double-pointed needles. When starting to knit, make sure the row of stitches is not twisted. Knit one round.

Begin pattern stitch:

Rows 1, 2, 3: *K5, bring yarn in front, sl3p, put yarn in back, repeat from * to end.

Rows 4 and 8: Knit.

Rounds 5, 6, 7: K1, *bring yarn to front, sl3p, return yarn to back, k5, repeat from * until 4 sts remain. K 4.

Repeat pattern 3 times. (24 rows)

Turning round: P first stitch, inserting needle in the row below to eliminate jog from turning. P1, k2, *p2 k2, repeat from * to end.

Work in k2, p2, ribbing for 2½" (6.5cm). Turn cuff and ribbing inside out by pulling work through the center of the triangle made by the double-pointed needles.

Sl1, k to end of round, inc 1. Place marker.

Next round:

K20 st, pm, inc 1, k1, inc 1, pm, knit to end of round. In this manner, inc 2 sts within markers every third round 6 times more. (15 gusset sts)

On the next round, run waste yarn through the thumb gusset stitches and tie it off. Using the backward loop method, cast on 1 st to close the gap between the thumb stitches and those for the hand. Continue knitting on 41 sts until hand measures 3½" (9cm) from the beginning of the stockinette section.

Skill level:	◖■■■▢
Materials:	
Yarn:	Heirloom 8 ply 107yd (98m)/ 1.75 oz (50g)
Color:	760 Red
Amount:	2 balls
Total yardage:	214yd (196m)
Needles:	One set of double pointed needles US 6 (4mm) or size to get gauge
Gauge:	22 sts and 30 rows = 4" (10cm) in St st.
Finished size:	Woman's medium to large (hand circumference 7½" (19cm)

Continue hand:
Pick up 32 sts held aside. Join yarn on last st before gap between hand and little finger. Pick up 2 sts along cast-on edge for little finger. (34 sts) Knit for ¼" (0.6 cm).

Ring finger:
Keep first 6 sts and last 6 sts on needles, and place remaining 22 sts on a length of waste yarn. Cast on 1 st to close gap between finger and hand. Knit on 13 sts until finger measures 2½" (6cm) long or desired length.

Next round: *K2 tog, repeat from * until 3 sts remain. K3tog. Cut yarn, leaving length of about 6" (15.25cm). Thread a tapestry needle with yarn end and run it twice through loops of stitches. Run yarn to inside of finger.

Middle finger:
Put first 5 sts and last 5 sts on needles. Pick up 2 sts along cast-on edge of ring finger and cast on 1 st, using backward loop, to close gap between back and front of finger. (13 sts) Knit even for 2¾" (7cm) or until desired length.

Next round: *K2 tog, repeat from * until 3 sts remain. K3 tog. Cut yarn, leaving length of about 6" (15.25cm). Thread a tapestry needle with yarn end and run it twice through loops of stitches. Run yarn to inside of finger.

Index finger:
Put remaining 12 sts on needles. Pick up 2 sts at base of middle finger. (14 sts) Work even until finger measures 2½" (6.5.cm) long or desired length.

Next round: *K2tog, repeat from * to end. Cut yarn, leaving 6" (15.25cm). Thread a tapestry needle with yarn end and run it twice through loops of sts. Run yarn to inside of finger.

Above
Here you can see the length of the elegant red gloves, and the contrast between the smooth stitches all over the hand area and the ladders on the turn back cuffs.

Begin little finger:
Next round: Work the first 5 sts and put next 32 sts on a length of waste yarn for the rest of the hand. Cast on 2 sts to close the gap between front and back sts of finger. K4 sts to end of round. (11 sts on little finger)
Knit until finger is 2" (5cm) or desired length.
Next round: *K2tog, repeat from * until 3 sts remain. K3 tog. Cut yarn, leaving a length of 6" (15.25cm). Thread a tapestry needle with yarn end and run it twice through loops of stitches. Run yarn to inside of finger.

Thumb:
Put gusset sts on needles and pick up 1 st along cast-on edge of hand. (16 sts)
Work until thumb measures 1¾"(4.5 cm) or desired length.

Next round: *K2 tog, repeat from * to end. Cut yarn, leaving length of about 6" (15.25 cm). Thread a tapestry needle with yarn end and run it twice through loops of stitches. Run yarn to inside of finger.

Right
These little pearlized heart shapes create a bright contrast to the red yarn used for the ladder pattern at the wrist.

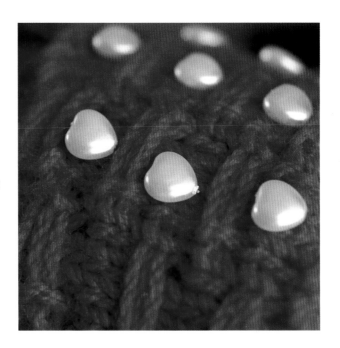

EFFORTLESS GLOVES AND MITTENS

If you have difficulty maintaining an even tension when you move from one double-pointed needle to the next, try varying the location of that stitch shift by knitting one or two extra stitches with your working needle.

For the best results, use double-pointed needles made of wood or bamboo. They have a surface tension that keeps the stitches in place better than slippery metal or plastic needles, especially when you have only a few stitches on the needles as in the finger area of your gloves.

The type of increase used for the thumb gusset will affect the overall look. For a neat finish, use a Make 1 (M1) increase, slanting to the left for the first gusset increase across the thumb stitches, and slanting to the right for the second increase. The lifted increase also works well for a thumb gusset. (See the increase techniques on page 18.) Whatever the increase technique you select, be sure to work the increases symmetrically.

To close the finger tips, draw the yarn through the remaining stitches twice to pad them and avoid leaving any holes.

For a good fit, measure the circumference of the hand with the hand lying flat.

Work the finger tip decreases when the knitting almost covers the fingernail.

To minimize gaps at the base of the fingers, pick up or cast on one or two more stitches than specified, then decrease the extras after one round.

When moving the stitches from a holder back onto the needles, begin at the stitch immediately preceding the gap between the finger just completed and the one you are now going to work.

When joining yarn at the base of fingers, leave long tails that can be used to close any holes or gaps that may have developed.

KIDS' STUFF

Making snowballs will be all the more satisfying for the young people in your life when they wear these color block mittens, which bring the colors of the sky down to earth. Better yet, it takes no time at all to knit them up.

INSTRUCTIONS

With color A, and double-pointed needles, cast on 28 (30, 32) sts and distribute as evenly as possible over three or four needles. When you start to knit, make sure the row of stitches is not twisted.

Color note: Alternate color A and color B every 8 (9, 10) rounds.

Work in k1, p1 ribbing for 2" (2¼", 2½") [5cm (5.7cm, 6.5cm)].
Change to St st and increase 1 st at the end of the next round. (29, 31, 33) sts)

Work thumb gusset: K14 (15, 16) sts, place marker, inc 1, k1, inc 1 pm, k to end of round.

In this manner, inc 2 sts within markers every 3 rounds 0 (2, 2) times and every four rounds 3 (2, 2) times. (Total gusset sts: 9, 11, 11)

K to gusset sts and place them on a length of waste yarn. Cast on 1 st to bridge gap between thumb and hand. Finish round. (29, 31, 33 sts) Work even until stockinette stitch section measures 3" (3½", 4") [7.6cm (9cm, 10cm)] or until it reaches tip of index finger.

Next round (all sizes): Decrease 1 st. (28, 30, 32 sts)

Skill level:	■ ■ □ □
Materials:	
Yarn:	Filatura di Crosa Primo 81yd (74m)/1.75oz (50g)
Color:	Color A, 292 pale blue
	Color B, 267 pale turquoise
Amount:	1 ball each A and B
Total yardage:	81yd (74m) for color A, 81yd (74m) for color B
Needles:	One set of double pointed needles US 7 (4.5mm) or size to obtain gauge
Gauge:	20 sts and 26 rows = 4" (10cm) in St st.
Size:	To fit children 2 to 4 (4 to 6, 6 to 8) years
Finished circumference:	5½" (6", 6½") [14cm, (15.25cm, 16.5cm)]

Mitten cap shaping:
Round 1: K1, [sl1, k1, psso], k 8 (9, 10), k2tog, k2, [sl1, k1, psso], k8, (9, 10) sts, k2tog, k1. (24, 26, 28 sts)

Round 2: K1, [sl1, k1, psso], k6, (7, 8), k2tog, k2, [sl1, k1, psso], k 6 (7, 8) sts, k2 tog, k1. (20, 22, 24 sts)

Round 3: K1, [sl1, k1, psso], k4, (5, 6), k2tog, k2, [sl1, k1, psso], k4, (5, 6) sts, k2tog, k1. (16, 18, 20 sts)

Round 4: k1, [sl1, k1, psso], k2 (3, 4), k2tog, k2, [sl1, k1, psso], k2 (3, 4), k2tog, k1. (12, 14, 16 sts.)

For medium and large sizes
Round 5: K1, [sl1, k1, psso], k1(2), k2 tog, k2, [sl1, k1, psso], k1 (2), k2tog, k1. (10, 12sts)

Final round for small and large sizes: K1, [sl1, k1, psso], k2tog, k2, [sl1, k1, psso], k2tog, k1.

Final round for medium size: k1, [sl1, k1, psso], k2tog, k1, [sl1, k1, psso], k2tog.
Run yarn twice through stitches. Bind off.

Thumb:
Put gusset stitches onto three double-pointed needles. Using color B, pick up one stitch from side of hand stitches to close gap between hand and thumb.
Total thumb stitches 10 (12, 12).

Work even until thumb measures ¾" (1", 1¼") [1.75cm, (2.5cm, 3.75cm)] or to middle of thumbnail.
Next round: *K2tog, repeat from * to end.
Cut yarn, thread tapestry needle and run through sts. Bind off.

Above
The color block pattern in this pair of mittens starts in the ribbing at the cuff.

Above
Lines of decreases lead to the tip of the mittens, where the yarn is run inside the remaining stitches.

Left
The hand of the mitten is knit in the round after stitches for the thumb are put aside. Using alternating thick bands of color makes for an interesting effect.

FINGERTIP FREEDOM

Have it both ways—the warmth of mittens and the convenience of gloves. Worked in the round, the mitten top grows out of stitches picked up along the back of the hand. Additional stitches are cast on to cross the palm and complete the circle.

INSTRUCTIONS

Cast on 34 (38, 40) sts.
When starting to knit, make sure the row of stitches is not twisted.
Work in k1,p1 ribbing for approx. 2½", (2¾", 2¾") [6.5cm (7cm, 7cm)].
Change to St st. At the end of first round inc 1 st for all sizes.

Thumb gusset: K 17,(19, 20,)sts, place marker, inc 1, k1, inc 1, pm, k to end of round.
Increase 2 sts within markers every third row 2 (4, 6) times more. Then inc. 2 sts within markers every 4 rounds 2 (1, 0) times. Total gusset sts: 11 (13, 15)

Note: Run waste yarn to the front and back on alternate stitches during the following round to mark line where thumb separates from hand. It will be useful later in determining where to pick up stitches for mitten top.

On next round, knit to gusset sts, place gusset sts on a length of waste yarn, Using the backward loop method, cast on 1 st to close the gap between the thumb stitches and those for the hand. Continue knitting on 35 (39, 41) sts until hand measures 3¼" (3½", 3¾") [8.5cm (9cm, 9.5cm)] from beginning of stockinette section.

Skill level:	◖■■■▢
Materials:	
Yarn:	Zara 100% Extrafine Merino wool 136.5yd (125m)/1.75oz/50g
Color:	For Color A: 1663 chocolate brown For Color B: 1728 cream For Color C: 1735 turquoise
Amount:	2 balls color A, 1 Ball color B, 1 ball Color C
Total yardage:	273yd (250m) for Color A, 136.5yd (125m) for Color B, 136.5yd (125m) for color C
Needles:	One set double-pointed US 6 (4mm) One set double-pointed US 7 (4.5mm)
Gauge:	20 sts and 28 rows = 4" in St st.
Finished size:	For children's 8 years to woman's small hand circumference 7" (18cm), medium 7½" (19cm), large 8" (20.5cm)

Begin little finger:
Next round: Work first 4 (5, 5) sts and put next 28 (30, 32) sts on a length of waste yarn for the rest of the hand. Cast on 1 (1, 1) st to close the gap between front and back stitches of finger. Continue knitting to end of round. 8 (10, 10) sts on little finger
Knit until finger is 1" (2.5cm) or desired length. Bind off.

Continue hand:
Pick up sts held aside. Join yarn on last st before gap between hand and little finger. Pick up 2 sts along cast-on edge for little finger. Total sts: 30, (32, 34). Knit for ¼" (0.6cm) for all sizes.

Ring finger:
Keep first 5 (6, 6) sts and last 5 (6, 6) sts on needles, and place remaining sts on length of waste yarn.
Cast on 1 st to close gap between finger and hand. Knit on 11 (13, 13) sts until finger is about 1¼" (3.2cm) or desired length.

Middle finger:
For all sizes, put first 5 sts and last 5 sts on needles. Pick up 2 sts along cast-on edge of ring finger and cast on 1 st, using backward loop, to close gap between back and front of finger (13 sts). K even for 1½" (3.8cm) or desired length. Bind off.

Index finger:
Put remaining 10 (10, 12) sts on needles. Pick up 1 (2, 2) sts at base of middle finger. 11 (12, 14) sts. Work even until finger measures 1¼" (3.2cm) or desired length.

Thumb:
Put gusset stitches on needles and pick up 1 st along cast-on edge of hand. 12 (14, 16) sts. Work until thumb measures 1¾" (4.5cm) or desired length.
Next round: *K2 tog, repeat from * to end.

Thread a tapestry needle with yarn end and run it twice through loops of stitches. Run yarn to inside of thumb.

Mitten top:
Note: It will be easier to work this section if you turn the half-fingers inside out, pushing them down into the hand.
Use US 7 (4.5mm) needles, or one size larger than used for glove portion.

About half way between the base of the little finger and the line of waste yarn marking the separation of the thumb gusset stitches from the hand (see note, above) run a length of waste yarn under one loop of each stitch across the back to mark pick-up line.
Until this point, both hands have been worked identically.

For left hand, pick up 18 (20, 21) sts across the back of the mitten, beginning at thumb side.
For right hand, pick up same number of sts across the back of the mitten, but begin below the little finger.

Next, put working needle in left hand and cast on 18 (20, 23) sts in cable or knit-on method. (Total 36, 40, 44 sts)

Round 1 : With A, knit 18 (20, 21) sts across back of hand. Attach B and k the first cast-on st. With A, put yarn in front, p1 and return yarn to back. With B, k1. Continue with both A and B in k1, p1 ribbing, as established, until end of round.

Next round: Begin working chart on Round 1. At the start of ribbing on the palm side of the mitten top, continue working ribbing in both A and B as established.

On round 3 of chart, discontinue ribbing and carry pattern all the way around mitten top. Work through round 14 of chart, or until piece is about 1½" shorter than desired length.

Shape top:
Round 1: K1, ssk, k12 (14, 16) k2tog, k2, ssk, k12, (14, 16), k2tog, k1.
Next round: Work even.
Round 3: K1, ssk, k10 (12,14), k2tog, k2, ssk, k10, (12, 14) k2tog, k1.
Next round: work even.
Round 5: K1, ssk, k8 (10, 12) k2tog, k2, ssk, k8 (10, 12) k2tog, k.
Work 1 round even.
Round 7: K1, ssk, k6, (8, 10) k2tog, k2, ssk, k6 (8, 10) k2tog, k1.
Work 1 round even.
Round 9: K1, ssk, k4 (6, 8) k2tog, k2, ssk, k4 (6,8), k2tog, k1.
Break yarn, leaving tail of at least 16" (40cm).
Graft stitches at top of mitten.

Glove Pattern

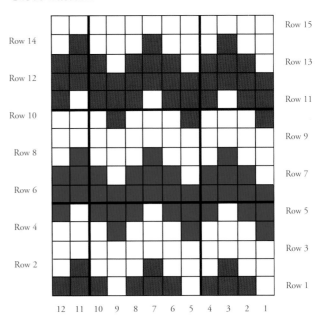

Row 14
Row 12
Row 10
Row 8
Row 6
Row 4
Row 2

Row 15
Row 13
Row 11
Row 9
Row 7
Row 5
Row 3
Row 1

12 11 10 9 8 7 6 5 4 3 2 1

Opposite Page and Below
The mitten top flips up onto the back of the hand whenever you need to free your fingers and, below, the mitten top, ringed with a zig-zag design, covers the fingers for warmth.

Glossary of Terms

In this list you will find most of the terms you will come across when you are reading a pattern.

A **Above markers:** Knitting worked after markers were placed in certain stitches

Above ribbing: Work done after last row of ribbing

Along neck: Used in describing a neckline where stitches are picked up

Around neck: Also used in describing a neckline where stitches are picked up [regardless of shape of neckline]

As established: Continue to work in sequence or pattern as previously positioned, to keep the continuity of the design or pattern

As foll: Work the following instructions

As for back; as for front: Work piece identical to the one mentioned in the instructions

Asterisks: * * Used to designate the beginning and often the end of sequences that are to be repeated

B **Back edge:** Any edge on the back piece of an item

C **Centimeter (cm):** Metric unit of measurement that often appears along with inches in gauge schematic on yarn labels, garment schematics, or some direction measurements. One centimeter is about .4 inches; 1 inch is about 2.54 centimeters.

D **Directions are for smallest size with larger sizes in parentheses:** In instructions given for more than one size, the smallest size is listed first, with the progressively larger sizes grouped within parentheses

Do not turn work: Keep the work facing in the same direction as the row just completed

E **Each side or each end:** Work according to the directions both at the beginning and at the end of a particular row

Ending with RS row or end with WS row: The work is finished when you have completed a right side (RS) or wrong side (WS) row

Every other row: When increasing or decreasing, leave one row between shaping rows

F **Fasten off:** To secure the stitches at the end of a bound-off row, when only the single last stitch remains, cut the yarn and draw the cut end through the loop of this last stitch, pulling the end to tighten the knit

Front edge: The center front edge of the front piece of a garment

G **Gauge:** Number of stitches and rows over one square inch, or a larger specified area of knitting, often a four-inch (10-centimetre) square

H **Hold in back of work or hold in front of work:** Applies to stitches on cable needle held in back or front of work as it faces you; found in cable and Aran patterns

I **Inc (number of) sts evenly across row:** Increase a specific number of stitches at even intervals across a row

In the same way or manner: Repeat the process previously described

K **K the knit sts and p the purl sts:** When a pattern has been established, work each stitch like the one below in the previous row as it faces you. A knit stitch on the right side looks like a purl stitch on the wrong side and vice versa. If the stitch now looks like a purl stitch on this row facing you, purl it (even though it was a knit stitch on the opposite side of the work).

Knitwise: Insert needle or work as if you were making a knit stitch

M **Make one (M 1):** Increase one stitch by lifting the horizontal strand between two existing stitches onto the left needle to form a loop; knit the loop, twisting it, to make the added stitch

Multiple of (number) sts plus (number): The number of stitches required for working a pattern for one repeat (the multiple), and any extra stitches at the ends to frame the pattern or make it symmetrical

P **Pattern repeat:** The number of stitches needed to work a pattern once

Place marker(s): Place a marker on the needle between stitches as a reminder to make an increase or decrease, indicate a pattern repeat, or some other change in the pattern

Place a marker in work: Mark a specific row or stitch with a safety pin or yarn for shaping or measurement (for length of armholes, for example)

Preparation row: A row that sets up a pattern stitch but is not part of the actual pattern

Purlwise: Insert needle or work as if you were making a purl stitch

R **Rep between *'s:** Repeat all the instructions from the first asterisk to the second one once more or as many times as indicated

Rep from *: Repeat all the instructions after the asterisk across the row or as many times as indicated, ending the rows as instructions say

Repeat from * around: Used when knitting with circular needles, this means to repeat the instructions after the asterisk until the end of the round, the point where the cast-on stitches were joined

Repeat from (numbered) row: Repeat previously worked instructions from the row with the designated number

Rep inc or rep dec: Repeat the increase or decrease as previously instructed

Rep (number) times more: Repeat the just-worked instructions as many times as designated

Reverse shaping: Used when pattern calls for two pieces that are mirror images of each other, as for right and left fronts

Right side: Refers to the right side of the finished garment when it is being worn [Right side of garment is not abbreviated as RS because it may be confused with RS of work below.]

Right side of work (RS): Refers to the outside of the garment, the part that shows when the garment is worn

Row 1 and all RS or odd-numbered rows: Used when all right-side rows, or all odd-numbered rows are worked the same way

Row 2 and all WS or even-numbered rows: Used when all wrong-side rows or all even-numbered rows are worked the same way

S **Same as:** Repeat the instructions given in another section of the pattern

Schematic: A scale drawing or diagram showing the measurements of all pieces of a project before it is assembled

Selvage st(s): An extra stitch (or stitches) at the sides of a piece used either to make a decorative edge or to making seaming easier

Slip markers: Move markers from left needle to right when you come to them to keep each one in the same position row after row

Swatch: A sample of knitting made to test gauge or try out a pattern or colors

T **Through (number) row:** Work up to and including the row with the specified number.

Total length: The length of a finished garment from top to bottom

Turn or turning: Transfer(ring) your work from right hand to left hand after completing a row. The tip of each needle changes direction in this transfer and the opposite side of your work now faces you. The yarn is in position on the left needle tip to begin work.

W **Weave in ends:** On the WS, work tails into stitches so they do not unravel and do not show on the outside of the garment

With the right side (RS) facing: The side of the work that will face outside on the completed item now faces you for the specific procedure, such as when you pick up stitches

With the wrong side (WS) facing: The side of the work that will face inward on the completed garment now faces you

GLOSSARY OF TERMS continued

Work even: Continue working in pattern without increasing or decreasing

Work to correspond: Work one piece, or side of a symmetrical shape, so that it is a mirror image of the other side

Working yarn: Yarn being used to form new stitches and drawn from a ball, skein, or bobbin

Wrong side of work (WS): The side of the finished garment that faces inward when the garment is worn

SKILL LEVELS FOR KNITTING AS USED IN PROJECTS

Beginner ◨☐☐▷
Projects for first-time knitters using basic knit and purl stitches. Minimal shaping.

Easy ◀◼☐▷
Projects using basic stitches, repetitive stitch patterns, simple color changes, and simple shaping and finishing.

Intermediate ◀◼◼▷
Projects with a variety of stitches, such as basic cables and lace, simple intarsia, double-pointed needles and knitting in the round needle techniques, mid-level shaping and finishing.

ABBREVIATIONS

[ ]	Work instructions within brackets as many times as indicated.
* *	Repeat instructions between asterisks as directed
*	Repeat instructions following the single asterisk as indicated.
alt	alternate, alternately
approx	approximately
beg	begin/beginning
bet	between
CC	contrasting color
cm	centimeter(s)
cn	cable needle
CO	cast on
cont	continue (ing)
dec	decrease, decreases, decreased, decreasing
dp	double-pointed needle(s)
foll	follow/follows/following
g	gram
inc	increase/increases/increasing
k	knit
k2tog	knit 2 stitches together
kwise	knitwise
lp(s)	loop(s)
m	meter
M1	make one stitch, an increase
MC	main color
mm	millimeter(s)
oz	ounce(s)
p	purl
pm	place marker
p2tog	purl 2 stitches together
Psso	pass slip stitch over
pwise	purlwise
rem	remain, remaining, remains.
Rev St st	reverse stockinette stitch
rnd(s)	round(s) in circular knitting
RS	right side
sc	single crochet

sk	skip
sl1, k1, psso	slip one stitch knitwise, knit 1, pass slip stitch over the knit stitch
sl1, k2 tog, psso	slip one stitch knitwise, knit 2 together, pass slip stitch over the 2 stitches knitted together
sl2, k1, p2sso	slip 2 stitches knitwise, knit next stitch, pass 2 slipped stitches over the knitted stitch
sl2, k2tog, p2sso	slip 2 stitches knitwise, knit 2 stitches together, pass 2 slipped stitches over the stitches that were knit together
sl	slip a stitch without working it
sl1k	slip 1 knitwise
sl1p	slip 1 purlwise
sl st	slip stitch
ssk	slip next 2 stitches knitwise individually from left to right needle,then insert tip of left needle through fronts of loops from right to left. Knit them.
st(s)	stitch or stitches
St st	stockinette stitch or stocking stitch
tbl	through the back loop
tog	together
WS	wrong side
wyib	with yarn in back
wyif	with yarn in front
yd(s)	yard(s)
yfwd	yarn forward
yo	yarn over
yon	yarn over needle

INDEX

ACKNOWLEDGMENTS

This book would not have been possible without my colleague Lynn Bryan, whose influence and direction were central in shaping the final product. Kim Conterio of Bella Yarns generously gave of her time as a sounding board. Thanks also go to Natalie Darmohraj at A Stitch Above, Louise Silverman at Sakonnet Purls, and Martha Demars of And the Beads Go On.

Thanks also to the following yarn companies who produce such lovely yarns to knit with:

Artyarns Inc. (www.artyarns.com), Berroco Inc. (www.berroco.co), Cascade Yarns (www.cascadeyarns.com), Classic Elite (www.classiceliteyarns.com), Trici and Chet at T. & C. Imports, distributors of Frog Tree Yarns, Debbie Bliss Yarns (www.knittingfever.com), Filatura di Crosa (www.tahkistacycharles.com), Green Mountain Spinnery (www.spinnery.com), Heirloom Easy Care (www.russisales.com), Jo Sharp Artful Yarns (www.jcacrafts.com), and Rowan Yarns (www.knitrowan.com).

Chris MacDonald, you are an organizer extraordinaire. And I am ever indebted to the knitters, chief among them Elaine Boyd, the mistress of lace, and the marathoner. Thanks also to Pat Lagalle in Hampstead, England. Many thanks also go to Anne and Marie Barylick, Laura Goldstein, Ann McGarry, Marcia Mullin, Deborah Peterson and Lindsay Woodel, without whom this book still wouldn't be finished!

Thanks, too, are owed to my doggie friends Hamish and Buddy, and to Margaret Nunzi of Hampstead, London, for letting us feature her cute Jack Russell dog. To Conny Jude, the creator of the illustrations, thank you for your patience.

Last but not least, many thanks to my husband, Larry, and sons Mike and Jeff for their continuing love and support.